Acknowledgements

My thanks to all those busy home-based entrepreneurs who were willing to answer my questions, and especially those I interviewed in depth for this book. I have learned so much from you about running a successful business, all the way from following dreams and developing great ideas to keeping finances straight and marketing products. I admire you. Thanks to Allen Wiseman for his computer support and to Marilyn Burns, Home-Based Business Specialist, for her help and all she has done for hundreds of entrepreneurs.

I especially thank Posy and Tom Lough, for encouraging me in this project. Thanks to Greg Johnson, my agent, for his encouragement, enthusiasm, and help. And to David Robie of Starburst Publishers, for catching the vision for *Home Business Happiness,* I am grateful.

Special thanks to my husband Holmes, who is a constant source of love and support.

Home Business HAPPINESS

Cheri Fuller

Home Business HAPPINESS

CHERI FULLER

STARBURST PUBLISHERS

P.O. Box 4123, Lancaster, Pennsylvania 17604

To schedule Author appearances write:
Author Appearances, Starburst Promotions, P.O. Box 4123
Lancaster, Pennsylvania 17604 or call (717) 293-0939

Credits:
Cover art by Terry Dugan Design

HOME BUSINESS HAPPINESS
Copyright © 1996 by Cheri Fuller
Published in association with Alive Communications, Inc.,
P.O. Box 49068, Colorado Springs, CO 80949
All rights reserved.

First Printing, April 1996

ISBN: 0-914984-70-5
Library of Congress Catalog Number 95-69732
Printed in the United States of America.

Contents

Introduction

Entrepreneurs Who Succeeded

In the following pages you will read the stories of women and men who followed their dreams, pursued their goals as home-based business people, and in the process kept *their* family financial ship afloat. If you think of home-based business owners as "hobbyists," think again! Several of these entrepreneurs have built businesses worth in the hundreds of thousands to a million dollars. All have experienced success and satisfaction, and all have encountered struggles.

To some, "success" is working as a team with a spouse in a unique counseling service to bring healing and wholeness to men and women. To another, success is solving a weight and diet problem and then helping others lead healthier lives. To the Leonards of California success is placing thousands of children in adoptive, loving homes while they raise six of their own.

To Floyd Culp, success is coming out of retirement to build a million-dollar business in his own backyard—literally. To a single mother, it was having a home-based accounting business to support her family. To a rural ranch wife, it was generating enough income through her monogramming business to put her children through college, then finding she had created an extremely lucrative business.

To Mary Hunt, success is sharing her passion, through her newsletter, for saving money and getting out of debt. And to Posy Lough, success was making enough income, through her cross-stitch kits, to help raise her son Kyser.

This book not only shares others' secrets of success. It tells what you need to know to begin a thriving home business of your own.

1

Home Business Happiness

Fuller Productions and
Holmes Fuller Design & Building

"He made it!" "She's successful!" "They are experiencing real happiness." What do you think of when you hear these terms: successful, happiness, "made it"? When we first embarked on our self-employed adventures—first my husband Holmes in 1978 with the opening of "The Woodworks," an antique and collectible shop which grew into freelance interior design work and later evolved into homebuilding, and then my exit a few years later from full-time teaching to home-based professional writing, we had three children under five years old.

Seventeen years later, Holmes continues in the design and building business from his home office and my freelance writing has grown into ten published books (eleven, counting this one), numerous magazine articles, a mail-order business, and a speaking career. At the same time, as home-based working parents, we have raised our three children: Justin, the oldest, has graduated from college and is married. Christopher, 21, is a college junior, and Alison, 19, a high school graduate.

Are we happy? successful? That all depends on your—or more precisely—*our* definition of success and happiness. We have kept the family ship afloat, amid good weather and raging storms, some that were so fierce they threatened to sink us all. We have developed our gifts and talents, and continue to find great joy in using our creativity. We have made mistakes and hopefully learned from them. We have been stretched immensely and continue growing and learning.

Of top priority to me, I was at home when the children arrived from school, and when they were ill, I was able to pick them up and head for the doctor's office. Both my husband and I were available to attend hundreds of the children's tennis matches, art shows, baseball and volleyball games, musical events, and track meets throughout elementary, junior high, and high school.

And last spring as our youngest child, Alison, in shiny red cap and gown walked across the stage to receive her diploma, I felt extremely grateful for the years of homeworking and the chance to "be there" for my children and still work full-time in a career I loved.

I've had opportunities to speak to parents across the country on one of my passions: how to motivate their children to achieve, find their talents, and help kids have better childhoods—something many desperately need. I've done hundreds of radio interviews from home (sometimes while stirring a pot of bean soup for dinner.)

I have made many friends along the way through networking with teachers, writers, parents, and readers of my books—in person, by e-mail, and telephone. I've met some incredible people—industrious, creative ones like the entrepreneurs you'll read about in this book.

It has not been an easy road, but it has been a *great adventure!* And as Alison's high school career closed and opened to a new phase of her life, (wow, it went fast!) I knew I wouldn't change a thing, even if I could, about the decision made years ago to leave the employment of others and "come home" to work as a writer.

What Is A Home-Based Business?

What is a home-based business? A home-based business is not just one whose base is in the home, but one that does quality work, the kind that brings self-respect.

One-hundred-five-year-old Sarah Delany, author of *Having Our Say* (NY: Bantam, 1994): "Doing quality work—

that's what brings you self-respect, and that's something folks seem mixed up about today. You hear all this talk about self-esteem or self-respect, as if it were something other people could give you. But what self-respect really means is knowing that you are a person of value, rather than thinking, 'I am special' in a self-congratulatory way. It means, 'I have potential. I think enough of myself to believe I can make a contribution to society.' It does not mean putting yourself first. A big part of self-respect is self-reliance, knowing that you can take care of yourself."

> **Oh, but man's reach should exceed his grasp,**
> **or what's a heaven for?**
> *—Robert Browning*

Whether you are one of the over 26 million persons already in the at-home work force in America (either full or part-time), or a person facing a possible lay-off, whether you are a mom wanting to be at home to raise your children, a senior citizen with talent and a great idea or product you'd like to market, or a teacher looking for a sideline business to make ends meet, *you have great potential.* My hope is that you will learn many things in *Home Business Happiness* stories and secrets of entrepreneurs—that will help *you* build a successful home business and take care of yourself and your family, not just now but for a lifetime.

With computers, fax machines, modems, on-line research networks, and other telecommunications that home-based businesses can tap into, the sky is the limit on the state-of-the-art marketing, networking, and production you can accomplish.

The Top Five Reasons Americans Are Turning to Home-based Businesses:

1. A tiring commute
2. Stress
3. Pressures of a large office
4. Lack of job recognition
5. Desire for more quality time at home[1]

Here's What I've Learned

We all have our working style, organizational, and time management styles, even if we don't sit down and plot it out. Perhaps you're a left-brained dominant "file" person, with a perfectly neat office. Or maybe you gravitate to the right-brained "piles" approach of office management. Whatever your style or business, here are some time-savers and working tips I've discovered along the way that can help you be more productive and experience more "job satisfaction":

- Do errands once a day. You lose a lot of time if you go out once to the grocery store to pick up a few things for dinner, another time to the post office, and then leave at 3:30 to pick up your children from school. Make one sweep, leaving early enough before carpool to stop at the post office, grocery store, and any other errands. Whenever possible, have your spouse pick up something on his/her way home that can save you a trip.

- When someone gives you a business card that you want to save, staple it on a roll-a-dex card and it's ready to add in alphabetical order in your desk file. This has helped me keep up with a lot of people and avoid losing their phone numbers.

- No matter how busy you are in your home business, don't skimp on exercise. Besides being great for you physically and keeping you fit, exercise stimulates mental activity, improves memory, and enhances your creativity.

I find there's nothing better than a brisk morning or evening walk at a nearby golf course (before or after the golfers make their rounds) or park. The change of scenery from the confines of the office is invigorating. Burnout begins to melt away. My mind is refreshed as I watch the ducks out of the corner of my eye or gaze at the multicolored pansies in a garden plot. For me, walking is the exercise of choice because I don't have to put on special clothes, or spend time driving to a gym—I can step out the door and go.

However, if it's pouring down rain or a cold Oklahoma north wind is blowing, I head for a local mall to walk.

It's very tempting when I have tight deadlines and work is piled up to the ceiling in my home office to skip exercise—but trust me, the time spent will be multiplied back to you in renewed energy, increased fitness and *brainpower.*

- I keep yellow (or hot pink) sticky notes in my office and if someone calls while I'm working on a project, I write down the request (send me your speaking flyer and topics, for example, or mail me a book). If I stop what I'm doing to address an envelope, write a note and enclose the requested materials, I get sidetracked and may lose valuable working time and concentration. Then the next day or whenever I have a block of time designated for correspondence, I fill the request or order.
- "TO Do" Lists are essential for staying on track with goals. I use them regularly.
- Fax instead of call to give information. Even better, e-mail your message. It saves both time and money.
- It helps tremendously if your spouse is supportive of your home business. What's even better if you are mutually supportive of each other's endeavors. In our case, since Holmes and I are both self-employed and our offices are at home, we have opportunities to help each other and work as a team. If he is not here, I answer his phone (or take messages off the joint answering machine), type occasional contracts for him, and consult with him on his projects. (I also cook dinner most of the time but he's great at calling out for pizza.)

Holmes answers the phone for me if I'm out of the office. And we do have separate offices, one upstairs and one downstairs. He is better at details, and he helps me set up my bookkeeping on my book orders, and mail-order business. He may throw in a load of laundry or unloads the dishwasher, in the course of his day. If he is going out, he mails both our correspondence, thus saving me a trip to the post office. The first year I worked as a freelance writer, after giving up my full-time teaching job, he supported me financially and cheered me on, applauding each small success and article acceptance to magazines. I can't say enough about how supportive he's been and how grateful I am.

Work as a team, use the gifts and talents you each possess, and you'll both get more accomplished. If you are a single parent, get your children involved and feeling part of the enterprise. There is a lot a child or teenager can do: for example, stuff envelopes for a mailing or assemble kits, put labels on jars or padded envelopes, and help out with housework.

I love what Henry David Thoreau said,

"If you have built castles in the air, your work need not be lost; now put the foundations under them."

In other words, reach for the stars, but learn all you need to know to build your home-based business on a strong foundation. The valuable information in the pages ahead will help you do just that.

2

The Best From the Heartland

Frontier Soups

From bean to brothy, chilled to hot; soups for all seasons, events, and appetites—that's "Frontier Soups, Inc," the home business that has flourished since the night Trisha Anderson prepared and sold out of the first 275 zip-lock bags full of bean soup mix for the local Junior League holiday bazaar.

When a friend asked, "Don't you have something for our Food Experiences booth?" Trisha had no idea that a business was about to be birthed. She prepared the bags of her bean soup with original mix of seasonings, and heated pots of the soup to be put in a crock-pot and tasted by people who would come by the booth. Since soup is a superb sampling product with the easy assistance of a crockpot, the tactic of "Try it, you'll like it!" worked.

Before the actual bazaar even started, her soup mixes sold out and she had to make up more of just the right beans, spices, and seasonings. In fact, all weekend she had to rush to keep up with the demand for her special blend of "Minnesota Heartland Soup." At the end of the weekend market, Anderson realized she had the product *and* the market vehicle to sell it.

How did this wonderful product develop? A former English major, Anderson's area of expertise did not start out in the culinary department. But a love of cooking did run in the family.

All In the Family

"My mom was a terrific cook," she explained. "With her creativity, she could combine scraps of just about anything and transform them into something wonderful. I grew up experiencing the fun of being in the kitchen." That interest led to experimenting with various soups. She served them to appreciative family and friends and shared her recipes with students she taught in a cooking and soup-making classes at the local community college.

She also gave the soup-mix-in-a-bag as gifts to friends and got terrific feedback. On the pre-sale night, she gave hot samples of the already field-tested soup and saw the bags of bean soup disappear—which showed her that apparently a lot of other people liked the soup!

Cooking Businesses

The busy pace of people's lives has created a big demand for wholesome food "like Mom used to make" and contributed to the success of many home-based cooking businesses. Consider these possibilities:

- Create homemade cookies or muffins (Who knows— you might be the next "Mrs. Fields")
- Teach cooking classes
- Consult on parties
- Cater dinners and parties, for individuals and businesses
- Cake Decorating
- Breadmaking
- Tap into the big trend and need people have for low-fat, nutritious foods by creating a dish or dessert that is tasty and healthy
- Writing cookbooks
- Make and market frozen entrees
- Create a new food product: a delicious ice cream sauce or a unique Salsa, for example
- Make and sell dried seasonings or herb dip mix

- Making wedding cakes and grooms cakes
- Present nutrition and cooking seminars for medical and legal auxiliaries and church groups.

Regardless of the cooking-related enterprise that you choose, follow these tips:

- Work in something you're talented at and interested in; or, as many business experts say, "Do what you love, and the money will follow."
- Start small: If you want to teach cooking classes, for instance, start out teaching one group, and learn as you go rather than biting off more than you can chew and getting overwhelmed
- Be willing to diversify and let your enterprise evolve. You may start off with one area (consulting for parties) and find that custom cakes or dip trays are needed. Be flexible and you will grow.
- Meet health department requirements by getting your kitchen approved (which will probably entail remodeling to meet requirements of a commercial kitchen) or by using a kitchen at your church or restaurant that has met health department certification requirements.
- Get the support of your family before beginning, especially if you'll be using the kitchen or family space until late hours of the morning icing cookies or assembling food-filled gift baskets for your customers.
- Carefully research all your costs before pricing your product. Many veteran cooks advise pricing your product as if you were a storefront location, so that if you do grow out of your home, you don't have to double or triple your prices due to increased overhead expenses.

Frontier's pouches of legumes, herbs, and seasonings are selling at bazaars and fairs from Orange County, California, to Lake County, Illinois, from Texas to New York. "It's a unique marketing technique," says Anderson. Unlike huge trade shows, local bazaars allow for a smaller showcase. Customers don't make purchases in massive bulk but buy just as much as they can carry home to their kitchens.

Frontier Soups, Inc., now sells over 300,000 bags of soup mixes each year and is a success story worth looking at—both for the principles we can learn about starting and growing a business and for Trisha's balanced approach to blending family and work.

How Does Your Business Grow?

Frontier Soups got off to a good early start, but Trisha did not go into debt to rapidly expand it. Instead, she planned slow, steady expansion by adding one new soup mix a year, such as:

- Dakota Territory Pioneer Soup (a beef, barley and bean blend)
- Idaho Outpost Potato Leek Soup (a chunky, country-style potato soup)
- Michigan Ski Country Chili (a blaze-of-glory bowl of chili)
- New Mexico Mesa Fiesta Soup

With the addition of the newest soup, New England Seaport Fisherman's Stew, Frontier Soups, Inc. now has a collection of thirteen soups, "The Best From America's Heartland," plus two herb seasoning packets. They also offer gift baskets for holiday giving and a new selection of pantry items. Trisha also writes a newsletter to customers entitled, "Frontier Stirrings: A Potpourri of Cooking Ideas From America's Heartland" which contains cooking hints, nutritional news, new product announcements, and holiday offerings.

"I had no idea that this would develop into something so big," says Trisha. But by following her interests and love for great soups, coupled with her instincts for survival, she grew a creative, productive, yet flexible career.

"I have always worked since I was 16, both to satisfy monetary and psychological needs. Starting this business in my home with endless support from my husband enabled me to both raise a family (three children, now aged 20, 17, and 14) and work," she adds.

Consider your personal hobbies, interests, and passions. Jot them down below and beside each, write the service or business that could spring from one or from a combination of two or more of them. Following your own interests is an important secret to success! What are your:

Use Your Interests As a Springboard to Success

- Hobbies
- Interests
- Passions

Best Advice From Frontier Soups

From Trisha's point of view, there's no question it's better to start slowly. So don't despise small beginnings! In the first stages, take on what you can handle and do it well. Take time for developing a top-quality product or service. And whether it's an unusual bread mix you've concocted or a dynamite Southwestern hot sauce—offer something *unique*. If your product is excellent, the business will grow.

Developing a product that taps into the trends is another one of Frontier's secrets of success. Today, with the emphasis on eating well for better health, hearty, homemade soups are enjoying a resurgence. In addition, women are busier today than ever before, many working at a full-time career in addition to child-rearing, carpooling, and household responsibilities. Frontier Soups prepares easily, keeps hot for latecomers, and is great for leftovers, just what a family needs.

Next, it's important that your product have something that *distinguishes it from the other products* out in the market. Frontier Soup mixes enabled the customer to add her own creativity to the soup pot and create a wonderful meal without spending hours and hours over the stove—thus the product was distinctive. And unlike the "instant" variety, these soups contain no salt, MSG or preservatives, and can be adapted easily to low-fat diets. They offer families an alternative to a steady diet of expensive carry-out products, fast food, or frozen dinners.

- To Trisha, the focus is:
- Having a *great* product
- Displaying it beautifully
- Keeping momentum for cooking and developing new products.

Trisha's enthusiasm for Frontier Soups, Inc., is contagious. Momentum is fueled by the joy of knowing she's making "home-made" and entertaining easier, thus improving the quality of life for many families. As she says, "Add a salad and loaf of French bread from your grocery bakery, and you have a terrific hot meal to serve to your family or guests." Just interviewing her convinced me I needed to try one of the soups!

The main focus of Anderson's effort now is focusing on markets, developing new products, and selling. She is constantly looking for great ideas and experimenting with new soup and seasoning recipes.

Home Business Tip— Testing Your Product

Testing and retesting your product to improve it is a vital step *before* you offer it to customers. When Frontier is developing a new soup, Trisha tries it out on her teenagers and husband, neighbors, employees, and friends. They taste, give feedback, and offer suggestions. From those suggestions, she makes changes and a new soup is developed, which is taste-tested and evaluated. Much time goes into making the best possible soup for each new mix, and by the time the product is "in the bag" it has been through many test kitchens.

Write down two or three groups of people who can test your product:

1.

2.

3.

You might create a response sheet your testers can use to offer feedback as they taste or try your new product.

Developing Your Market

Is there a market for your product? With any product, as important as the quality of the product is *finding the vehicle for selling it*—the best ways to distribute it and let potential customers know about it. Identifying *your* target markets is essential. "My business definitely grew as a result of plugging into networks of largely female organizations such as women's boards of schools, hospitals, and Junior Leagues across the country," says Anderson. Women's organizations were her primary market.

To develop the primary market in the beginning stages of the business, Trisha drove to holiday markets in Chicago, Milwaukee, Michigan, and St. Louis. Once there, she set up her booth, thawed out and heated her soup, sold for two or three days, and then came home. Sales were brisk at each market.

Soon help was needed. Friends pitched in with assembling the soup mixes in bags. Her children did some packing and tying bows. Husband Jim covered the home front when she went on the road to do a show, and offered his saavy business advice when it was needed. In addition, she had to hire part-time and then full-time employees.

Expanding the Primary Market and Developing Secondary Markets

Frontier Soups, Inc., now does about 45 markets a year. Trisha does three or four of the shows herself, and all the other shows are managed by reps or women close to the location of the market. A Virginia woman presents at all their East Coast shows. A Denver woman sells in Denver, Dallas, and other regional markets in that part of the country.

From the Holiday Market Circuit came a mailing list for direct mail sales because people who bought the soups at the markets wanted to order their favorite soup mixes throughout the year until the Frontier Soups booth came back to their area.

From this vehicle developed their selling to Specialty Food Stores across the country, including Marshall Field's Gourmet Stores and many others. People in a specific area of the country asked a local store to carry the soup mixes for their convenience. Thus the wholesale part of the business started—the segment of the business that makes everything else work.

As Trisha Anderson explains, "It's the wholesale business that keeps us in a strong position all year. We had to sell more soup throughout the year to be able to have the inventory and man-power to prepare and pack ahead for the super-busy seasonal rush that occurs from October through Christmas." To handle the inventory, Frontier had to move out of the Anderson home and into a small warehouse, and then eventually a larger warehouse.

The wholesale business works in tandem with the show circuit and mail-order business Anderson has developed. And to handle the year-round mail and phone order business, wholesale business, and holiday market circuit in the fall of each year, extra employees were hired. Besides Trisha, the administrator, and a steady labor force of women to assemble the soup packages, during the "seasonal blimp" in the fall, they bring in friend and "friends of friends" from September to December to assemble, fill orders, cook and freeze the "bricks" of soup which will be shipped out in coolers to the shows.

The three segments of Frontier Soups: *retail selling at markets, direct mail sales,* and *wholesale sales,* keep the business with a stable and slowly expanding customer base all year.

Diversify Your Markets!

Think about possible secondary markets for your product and list here:

1.

2.

3.

**"The door of success swings on
the hinges of obstacles."**

—*Anonymous*

Approaching Problems—
Challenge or Catalyst for Growth?

One of the strengths of Frontier Soup's business is Trisha's approach to problems. "Problems are definitely *not* the worst things. They can move you forward," she says. Don't think "Oh, not another problem—this will ruin me!" See problems, instead, as a challenge and a catalyst for improvement. Although there are bigger problems now than when Frontier Soups started and more risk involved, that's what Trisha loves—the challenges and the creative side of problem-solving.

For instance, it was a big decision to move from the smaller warehouse to a bigger one they now occupy, but they had to have more space. To make that and other decisions, she employs a team decision-making process. Her husband worked on the financial planning and cash flow, giving her vital behind-the-scenes information. The women on her administrative staff discussed and participated in the decision and brainstormed on alternatives. The decision made to lease a bigger space enabled them to pack ahead for the holiday rush and the 45 markets on the circuit, to sell to wholesalers, and to expand their mail-order business.

To order "Frontier Stirrings" newsletter or the order form for soups and seasonings from the Heartland, call 1-800-253-0550.

3

Starting a Newsletter That Succeeds

The Story of Cheapskate Monthly

Want to hear a great home business success story? As Mary Hunt says, "It all started with one innocent gasoline credit card." That first credit led Mary and her husband Harold to the land of consumer debt devastation, where 12 years and 28 credit cards later, she had run up consumer debts totalling more than $100,000 (and this did not include the house mortgage).

But the story doesn't stop there in the pit of despair—it just begins there. Finally realizing the awful consequences of her cavalier attitude toward money and credit, Mary wanted to change. She not only stopped her compulsive spending; she vowed that if God would supply a way, she would do everything in her power to reverse the terrible process and get out of debt. Mary took a job managing industrial parks in order to begin to chip away at their debts. For a year, Harold stayed home with their boys in the role of "Mr. Mom". Mary and Harold cut up all the credit cards and began budgeting and skrimping in every creative way they could find.

Several years later (nine to be exact), Mary and Harold were still hacking away at the debt, but were frustrated at how slowly the payoff was going. She decided that she wanted to make a difference in the lives of others, so they could avoid the painful journey from the devastating debt she had experienced. Due to the fact that the 1991 California real estate market was going downhill, Mary began looking for a side-line business.

"The response came like a bolt from the heavens. I will never forget it," says Mary. Harold and I were out running errands one Saturday morning. Suddenly, without any warning, I threw up my hands and shouted, 'That's it! I'll publish a *newsletter!*'"

Mary had three requirements for any side business she started. It had to be a business that:

- Needed no cash to start; that meant no franchises
- Provided some mobility. They could move the business if they wanted, whereas with commercial real estate she was tied to California
- Did not require any inventory

The newsletter idea fit all three of these criteria. "I couldn't come up with anything that really excited me until I thought of a newsletter. I could do it at home, in the car on my way to work, anywhere there was a post office!" Although she had had no formal training in writing, Mary was skilled at writing contracts and business letters, drafting the proper language so all parties would understand.

Publishing a newsletter was also ideal because she could do it in addition to her real estate job. She could start with the equipment and knowledge she already had. And she could do all of the writing and publishing right in her home, and operate out of their existing post office box.

She decided that the newsletter needed a subject. What about the lessons she had learned about spending less, cutting back, saving more and paying off mountains of debt to share with her subscribers? Says Mary, "We had learned to do that in the nine years of frugality and skrimping. We could teach others to do the same!" So with enthusiasm, a whole lot of trust and faith, and a clear focus for her newsletter, Mary began her home-based publishing venture.

The Birth of Cheapskate Monthly

On January 1, 1992, *Cheapskate Monthly* entered the world, with the concept that it is possible to live within one's means without sacrificing dignity and style. Mary packed its pages with first person articles on subjects ranging from insurance policies to car leasing, discount shopping to coupons, all written by herself. She wrote articles like "How I Cut My Food Bill by Over 25% (And the Kids Never Knew)" and shared how to avoid "perma-

> *Don't Sit Around and Talk About What You Are Going To Do— Do It!*

debt" (increasing credit card balances). She also included thrifty ideas and just plain "fun stuff" about finances.

To cover stamps and mailing, Mary began accepting subscriptions sight-unseen to generate money up front. The first issue was printed on her own copy machine, so she didn't go to a printer until after the fourth month of publishing. The first 4000 copies of that premiere issue went to pre-sold subscriptions to pay for the copying costs. She had no idea of the tremendous response that would follow!

Here are some alternatives if you don't have a computer:

- You can rent time at Kinko's or a quick-print shop
- Go to a university computer lab
- Use a friend's computer

> *Money-Saving Tip*
>
> *Don't Spend a Dime Until You Have To!*

"Being naive, I thought there was a slight possibility that a few people out there had experienced financial difficulties like we had," says Mary. "The truth I quickly learned is that almost everyone has some problems managing money, and has made a credit card or bank error."

Also, Mary at first thought that women—probably young, newly married, and trying to make ends meet—were her primary audience. She soon realized that the audience for *Cheapskate Monthly* was equally split between men and women, and included lots of professionals—doctors, lawyers, engineers—not just stay-at-home moms trying to balance their budget. "It's for everyone who uses money!" she adds.

As thousands of copies made their way across the U.S. and Canada, positive responses began pouring in. Clearly, people everywhere are facing economic hardships. Consumer debt is a problem of nearly epidemic proportions, and people are in need of solutions.

Today, through *Cheapskate Monthly,* Mary continues full-time on her campaign to help people live frugally and responsibly within their means. Mary also publishes two more newsletters, *Beyond Home Improvement* (with a focus on fixing everything in and around the house, car, etc.) and a newsletter focusing on wise investing entitled *Investing for Rookies.* She writes financial columns in *Single Parent* magazine and Good Morning America *Extra,* speaks and does interviews all over the nation. This spendthrift-turned-cheapskate, who was looking for a business, discovered a whole new world and ways to help people she never dreamed of. And along the way, her family became totally debt-free.

Basics on Starting a Newsletter

Whatever your field—whether you are a mystery writer, run a kitchen tune-up business, or are a home-based CPA or educational consultant, writing a newsletter can serve several purposes including:

- Give you and your business visibility
- Give you credibility
- Expand your base of customers and clients

But as good as your newsletter idea may be, it needs wise start-up and management all the way, from the selection of your title to keeping track of your subscribers. Many newsletters are started each year with great intentions, but just as many fail.

Here are some ways to publish a successful newsletter on a shoestring:

Choose your newsletter's subject matter carefully. When Mary began *Cheapskate Monthly,* she hit a vein. The economy was in a decline; people were struggling financially. As you are choosing your newsletter's focus, study the newspaper headlines and peruse magazines to see what is most important to people, what their problems are. Find a trend and tap into it.

In addition, consider the breadth of your topic. If the topic is too narrow, your audience will be limited and you risk running out of material. If the topic is too broad, the media may pass you by. Media is always searching out specific topics. An ideal topic is relevant to large segments of people and of current interest.

Pick a topic you are very passionate about. The Middle East may be a recurring, important topic, but if you are not passionate about it, steer clear. One of the reasons for *Cheapskate Monthly's* success is the publisher's passion for the subject. It is written in a lively, enthusiastic style that reflects Mary's passion for saving money, staying out of debt, and helping others do the same. Next most important, the topic needs to reflect your expertise and knowledge. What are you passionate about? What are your particular fields of expertise?

Pick a dynamite title. Once you decide on your focus and subject matter, pick a title that hooks your potential reader and builds interest, a title that is simple but has a lot of punch. Most of all, let it reflect your mission. (You should be able to state your mission in one simple sentence—this will help you zero in on your topic).

Mary wanted a title that had enough zing and zip to it to create curiosity. She took a negative term like *cheapskate* and turned it into something fun, something positive: a financially responsible person.

A successful newsletter is well-researched. One of the biggest reasons for newsletter failure is a lack of research. Set a high standard of excellence for your newsletter, both in content and form—no typos (Proofread! Proofread! Then have the sharpest grammar and spelling friend you know proofread again). "Don't insult your reader," says Mary. "You don't have to know everything, but the more research you do, the better." Always take the

Study newsletter design. Collect newsletters and study them: what is good about each one? Why do you love one and get bored with another? What grabs your attention in certain newsletters? Look in the Reference Section of your library for *Newsletters in Print* (Robert Huffman and John Krol, Editors, Gale Research, Inc.) and you will find the names and addresses of thousands of newsletters in the U.S. Write or call for sample copies of newsletters, many of which are free, and learn all you can.

Three excellent resources to read before launching your newsletter are:

Newsletters from the Desktop, Joe Grossman,
(Ventana Press) $24.95 gives lots of information on how to lay
out a good newsletter, type fonts to use, etc.

The PC is Not a Typewriter, Robin Williams
(Peachpit Press) $9.95

The MAC is Not a Typewriter, Robin Williams
(Peachpit Press) $9.95

Mary advises that you find a great layout and stick with it. "If your newsletter is not attractive and compelling in design, your audience won't be engaged."

Copyrighting Concerns. A newsletter qualifies to be copyrighted through the U.S. Copyright Office. Putting a ©copyright sign does not give you any recourse if someone copied you and used the material in your newsletter without permission **unless it is registered.** To be protected, each issue has to be copyrighted. For a copyright form, write to:

The United States Copyright Office
The Library of Congress
Washington, D.C. 20559

After receiving the application form, complete all necessary spaces, send a nonrefundable $20 filing fee in check or money order payable to "Register of Copyrights," along with the material to be copyrighted.

In addition, you may want to trademark your newsletter's name to protect it from being copied. Mary obtained a trademark for the title *Cheapskate Monthly,* used in connection with the name to protect it from being copied. Mary obtained a trademark for the title *Cheapskate Monthly,* used in connection with the newsletter subject of frugality. To register and trademark a name costs approximately $200 and takes two years, but you are protected from the date of application.

More Legal Matters. Once you produce and distribute your first issue, you are a publisher and an editor. Freedom of the Press entitles you to self-publish your newsletter without any legal licensing. You do need a permit for being in business, and need to check your county zoning regulations for being in business generally. But there is no law that designates what newsletters must consist of.

Count the Cost. Not just the cost in terms of stamps, printing, etc., but the cost in terms of commitment and time. "It's a tremendous commitment to publish a newsletter," confides Mary. "You're committed for the next twelve months, and two years if the subscriptions run twenty-four months. I take the responsibility seriously."

Caution: The laws on mail order are very tight. You have 30 days to notify the subscribers and refund all their money if your newsletter stops publication or if you don't deliver an equal or better product or you can be guilty of mail fraud.

The Federal Trade Commission has numerous free publications to assist you in establishing lawful advertising campaigns. Two helpful booklets with guidelines are *A Business Guide to the Federal Trade Commission's Mail Order Rule,* and *FTC Guide Concerning the Use of the Word "Free" and Similar Representations.* These free booklets and a catalog of other publications can be ordered from:

> The Federal Trade Commission
> Room 130
> Washington, D.C. 20580
> (202) 326-2222

You also need to also determine your basic start-up costs including equipment, printing, mailing, and advertising.

Besides writing the content, doing layout, proofing, negotiating small those first three months, it took only one-eighth to one-fourth of her time, but as *Cheapskate Monthly* grew, it became a bigger job. Because she loves helping people live responsibly with their finances, the newsletter continues to be a project she considered "fun" as month after month the issues have been produced and distributed on deadline to her growing mailing list of subscribers.

"I did my own layout; I always loved rubber cement, cutting and pasting and writing down orders as a child—instead of playing with dolls." So when she had to devote more time to publicity, answering mail, filling orders, and getting ready for the next deadline because of a large readership, it was enjoyable instead of a burden.

Deadlines, Deadlines. If you are not comfortable with deadlines, avoid producing a newsletter and choose a different kind of home business. However, if you work best under deadlines, as Mary does, and thrive in a challenge, this may be just the niche for you. How often these deadlines come is your choice, but **successful newsletters come out every month,** with each issue arriving **on time,** not drifting into the subscribers' mailboxes a few weeks late. Send it out less often (such as every other month,or four times a year) and your subscribers tend to forget about the newsletter; their interest wanes and so do subscriptions.

Pricing your newsletter at a competitive rate is also important, and you can check to see what other newsletters comparable to yours cost. Mary decided to offer much more than the $20 to $30-and-up newsletters gave subscribers at a beginning price of $12.95 for eight pages (perfect for aspiring cheapskates!). *Cheapskate Monthly* now has 12 pages in each issue for a yearly rate of $15.95.

Use Bulk Mail. If you have at least 200 pieces of mail per newsletter mailing, you will save money by using bulk mail. Check with your local post office on requirements, how to prepare the pieces of mail by zip code, and the yearly bulk mail permit (which runs $75 to $89). The postmaster can give you a complete booklet on the how-to's of using bulk mail. Read it before you prepare and sort your mail.

on the how-to's of using bulk mail. Read it before you prepare and sort your mail.

"Even if you have only a few subscribers," says Mary, "you can easily make up the 200 by sending complimentary issues to media contacts. Bulk mail can be rather slow unless you prepare everything with zip code + four digits and barcodes" (a simple process that requires software). If you do this preparation for the post office, you are given discounts on the postage and your pieces zip through the system. *Cheapskate Monthly* averages $.209 per piece instead of $.55 per piece if sent first class mail.

Act like a professional. "I decided I was going to act like my business was a large, able-to-meet-your-needs kind of operation from the very beginning," says Mary, who answered the office phone in a professional manner. She kept circulation statistics to herself. "That's private information, except for an advertiser." she adds. If asked, she replies, "I'm sorry, that's a number I can't share with you; but by the end of the year, we hope to be in every state, Canada, Mexico, Hong Kong, etc."

In addition, part of being professional is **Learning How to Work with the Media.**

"Once you've published an issue, you are a publisher, so act like one," says Mary. "When you call an editor or publisher, you are a peer, and not a begging peon." Here are some effective strategies for working with the media:

- Elevate yourself to the highest level of professialism. Have letterhead, envelopes, and business cards.
- Present material the way newspaper editors need it: in a Press Release. Avoid an amateur press release. If you don't know how, find someone who's worked in the publishing business to

Tips on Working With the Media for Free Publicity

- Offer your services. "I volunteered, got friendly with the *Good Morning America* newsletter editor and said, 'If you need anything, I'll be glad to help.' It paid off in eventually being chosen to write a regular column for their publication. Also, volunteer to speak at community luncheons and meetings, and ask for permission to promote your newsletter.

- Request review copies of books you can review in your newsletter or use in your business. "Refer to yourself as an editor because you are! Publishers will respect that," says Mary.

The newsletter *Cheapskate Monthly* was so successful that it spawned a mail-order business in which Mary now offers her books, tapes, and money-saving gadgets. If you start a mail-order business as a side to the newsletter or any other business, here are three important tips to remember:

1. **Respond immediately to orders**. The shorter the time between the moment your customer makes a decision to purchase your product and the time it arrives in the mail, the happier the customer. Happy customers are repeat customers.

2. **Exceed your customer's expectations.** This does not mean to underrate what your offer, but always strive to give far more than is expected. This means your descriptions and explanations of the product should be honest and very complimentary but never misleading and never more than you can deliver.

3. **Always remain a fragrance; never become an odor.** Keep in touch with your clients, but do not badger them. Make your services and products available, keep in touch regularly but never take advantage of the trust that customer has placed in you. Treat each customer as a true friend whether they ever order or not.

Actually, these tips apply to dealing with customers in any business, not just mail-order or newsletters, even friendships and parenting.

Actually, these tips apply to dealing with customers in any business, not just mail-order or newsletters, even friendships and parenting.

I consulted with Mary about ways we could save money in our home offices and discovered some "cheapskate" strategies any home business person can profit from:

- Fax instead of phone; it's cheaper. Even less expensive is to e-mail. Talk may be cheap; but not over long-distance!

Money-Saving Tips in Your Home Office

- When you must call long-distance, first check the 800 directory assistance at 1-800-555-1212 to see if the business has a toll-free number (even the 800 directory assistance is free). If you must call long-distance, aim for the person's lunch time and leave a message; then the conversation is on their nickel.

- Don't go into debt for new equipment if you can use what you have, and don't upgrade until absolutely necessary. "A lady called me and said, 'I went into debt $10,000 for a new Mac and color printer, etc., so can you tell me how I start a newsletter?" Use what equipment you have.

- Shop around to get the very best prices on printing, paper goods, padded envelopes, everything you use regularly. For anything you use regularly in large quantity, save money by buying in bulk. If you send out many products, for example, consider buying your padded mailing envelopes from the manufacturer instead of an office supply and you will save money.
  Always ask for cash discounts. Most of your suppliers are used to carrying their accounts for at least 30 days. If you pay cash up front you can usually get a discount.

- Don't hire employees until you absolutely have to.

4

The Sky Is the Limit: at Any Age

Aircraft & Industrial Services

Floyd and Margaret Culp, at an age that many people are heading for the rocking chair or golf course, are the most industrious entrepreneurs I know. In fact, they are busy helping other people of all ages enjoy the challenge and benefits of available to people who want to work from their homes. "I see nothing more sad than experienced and knowledgeable people who retire and are bored to death," says Floyd, 69. His wife Margaret adds that Floyd is a happy workaholic who would never be content "doing nothing."

Thus, after he retired after 18 years as Claremore, Oklahoma's Parks and Recreation Director, Floyd looked around for a new enterprise he and Margaret could partner. Margaret's interest in planting and growing things led them first to consider operating a greenhouse. After giving up that plan as "too seasonal," they turned to another lifelong interest—airplanes.

As a hobby since college days, Floyd bought antique and classic airplanes, and one at a time, rebuilt and flew them. He sold one, bought another, restored it, flew it, and then sold it. He had a commercial pilot's license. He also had an aircraft and power plant mechanic license and had experience as an aerial photographer. Yet, the Culps had no idea that Floyd's hobby would turn into a big business.

In preparation for retirement, the Culps had built a 32' x 32' metal building on their rural property big enough to hold an airplane, with the idea of continuing small aircraft repair. Their homeplace was a perfect site from which to operate almost any kind of business. Nestled at the bottom of a canyon on ten country acres just west of Claremore, Oklahoma, they had a water well and natural gas well which provided heat and water source for both home and business.

The Culps eventually had an acre and a quarter rezoned to "Light Industrial" by going to the county planning commission and informing them of their business and what they wanted to do. "We wanted to do what was right and follow all zoning regulations," Floyd says. They were led through the paperwork, submitted an application, and were granted a hearing. One neighbor protested the rezoning because he didn't understand what they were doing in their business; however, he withdrew his protest when he had more information. After the hearing, they were granted the change in zoning to "Light Industrial."

Zoning Ordinances

When you start a home-based business, check the zoning ordinances that govern home-based businesses in your area. The city hall, court house, or local library has zoning information.

Find out what your neighborhood is zoned for and what restrictions apply. Property is usually zoned in one of four classifications: Residential, Commercial, Industrial, or Agricultural.

Since most restrictions were defined thirty years ago to protect neighborhoods from smoke, dirt, and hazards of factories, the zoning ordinances may not recognize the high-tech, service-oriented businesses of today.

If you find your home is restricted from operating a business, consider these five options:

1. Adjust your business to meet the restrictions, such as no advertising in the yard, not having customers come to your door, or hiring employees to work at your home other than immediate family. If this is the case, you could contract with

an outside service for work you need done, or deliver gift baskets instead of having customers pick them up.

2. Apply for a variance or use permit from the zoning regulator to allow you to use your home for business. Getting a variance may be difficult and expensive.

3. Since most zoning codes regarding home businesses are outdated, work toward changing local zoning ordinances. This process will take time and you may meet resistance, but more and more cities and counties across the U.S. are gradually changing zoning regulations to recognize the positive economic development resulting from the increase in home businesses.

4. Some home-based businesses ignore the local zoning ordinances, but you may have to pay a fine or have to alter or close your business if cited.

5. If you are on the search for a new residence, check city zoning codes, homeowner's associations and property abstracts for restrictions that apply to the property *Before You Sign the Contract to Buy.*[2]

Using Prior Skills To Develop a New Business

The Culps thought Floyd might put his metal fabricating skills to use as a home-based business. They formed Aircraft and Industrial Services (AIS) in February of 1990 and did some private airplane repair contracting work; however, airplanes are so expensive, that soon there wasn't much work available.

Right before Floyd's retirement, in November, 1990, Margaret, active in the local Extension Center Homemaker's Group, invited him to go to a meeting about home-based businesses. At the meeting, the speaker discussed government contracting and the need for small businesses to bid on Defense Department contracts for manufactured airplane parts. Later, Floyd visited with the speaker in his office and as he says, "He sold us on the idea to be government contractors."

There was a lot to learn, much paperwork and many specifications to follow, including learning about military packaging. But with advice and help on getting the paperwork and quality control done from advisers at the Bid Assistance Center at Rose State College, AIS bid on their first Department of Defense contract in January, 1991. They were awarded that contract in February, 1991, for a small part for a B-52 jet for Tinker Air Force Base in Oklahoma. The amount of the order was $2,496.88. "With all the help we had getting started and all the resources available, we found it no problem to be Defense Department Contractors," explains Culp. He gives much credit to the Oklahoma Home-Based Business Association and advisors throughout the state at the Business Assistance Center and Vo-Tech Centers for showing him the right steps to take.

Although they were a brand new business with no credibility or history, when the Culps told prospective customers they were prime contractors for the Defense Department, they gained credibility. Consulting with one of their advisors at the Northeast Area Vo-Tech, the Culps decided they needed to balance their government contract work with commercial contracts. They connected with an organization called the Oklahoma Manufacturer's Exchange Center, whose purpose is to tie larger manufacturers with small manufacturers in order to produce and supply things that are being done out of state.

Soon after, the Culps attended a seminar and learned of an industrial need for metal brackets that hold pipes distributing natural gas. They bid on the contract, helped the company design the part, and began manufacturing brackets at the rate of 300-400 per month. As the natural gas company expanded their market at a steady rate of 10–20% per year, AIS continued to be the sole supplier for the part, producing approximately 2,000 per month by 1993. When the company was bought by an international company based in Switzerland in 1994, the demand for the bracket went crazy. Sales from that one part were over $200,000 for 1995. In fact, the Culps' industrial business is so busy that since 1994 they have had little time to bid on government contracts.

Passing On The Benefits

The benefits of their home-based business are many. Not only does AIS provide company cars, delivery vehicles, insurance and health benefits for themselves and their four employees, but the Culps can work as much or as little as they like. They own the building and land that the business sits on, and they are not in any debt.

Close proximity to work is another of the benefits. "I have a three-minute walk to the shop from the house on a pretty spring day, or thirty seconds when the cold wind or rain is blowing," smiles Culp. "It's a lot of fun." They thrive on the challenge and the creativity, and look for new ways to expand their enterprise.

Floyd and Margaret Culp are not just interested in benefitting their own pocketbooks and lives, although AIS is thriving business. (Aircraft and Industrial Services receives a daily list of 50–100 bid openings for just the type of work they do. They are prime contractors for some, and sub-contract other jobs out.) The Culps are also focusing on helping other people get motivated about starting home-based businesses as government and industrial contractors. Floyd feels a particular concern for employees laid off by aircraft companies. "We don't know why more people don't get involved in what we are doing," Floyd says. "I realize that people who have worked for a company and received a set salary, company benefits, and vacations have a hard time imagining being individual contractors. They've been told what to do for so long they often have difficulty taking a risk and saying 'I can do it.' "

"But I know it can be done because we did it," he adds. The business is out there if you're self-motivated; there are many contracts waiting for someone to bid on them—contracts for airplane parts, truck parts, and items like the hydraulic jack-screw for the Defense Construction Supply Center in Ohio that AIS produced and sold. "That was real simple to make." Culp says you can get quite simple or complex items to make, and feels that when layoffs in the aircraft or other industries take place, there is an abundance of work out there for self-starters.

And all the technical support is available through Vo-Tech

centers and Business Assistance Centers. You do need computer knowledge so that you can use the computer hardware and software to download the Commerce Business Daily from the product codes you are interested in. It also helps to have past experience, but you don't have to, he adds. Not all the products needed are from metal shops. For example, some items that are needed are fabric items, like a tail-roter cover for a helicopter made from heavy fabric. This product can be sewn on a commercial sewing machine. Almost every trade or skill is covered by things the government needs to buy.

Creating a New Product To Market

Although the industrial and Defense Department work continues, the Culps have entered into another phase of entrepreneurship: creating and distributing their own original products. From making the brackets, they used many large sheets of metal and had scraps by the dozen. Margaret, an avid gardener, was frustrated at the poor quality of the flowerbed edging available at stores (most of which was plastic). So they brainstormed about how to create a durable metal edging.

With his twelve-gauge steel waste pieces, Floyd set to work and created a metal edging that can be shaped and notched to fit together and form edging in a variety of sizes and shapes, including an octagon shape. The edging is attractive, easy to work with, and lasting. A housewife or anyone can assemble and use around lightposts, garden plots, or straight edging for sidewalks. Nursery owners say their metal edging is far better than what's available, and word began to spread.

Soon customers showed up at their shop doorstep wanting the buy the edging they had heard about—"Orna-Metal Ironworks by the Village Blacksmith," the name the Culps came up with for their ornamental metal works products. They also developed a line of durable, high-quality "Orna-Metal Ironworks" lawn and garden furniture. That name is now trademarked and registered, an important step to take with a new product. (See Seeking aTtrademark.)

A trademark is "a name, symbol, design, device, or word, or

any combination thereof, used by a merchant or manufacturer to identify his goods and distinguish them from those made or sold by others."[3]

Trademarks prevent one company or manufacturer from taking advantage of the reputation and name of another company. A trademark may consist of a word or phrase, a person's name, a symbol, picture, or a combination of these identifications. A registered trademark appears in an R with a circle around it after each use of the trademark word or symbol. A trademark that is in the process of being registered or merely being claimed appears with the letters TM.

What can be protected under a trademark? Brand names, trade names such as the Culps' "Orna-metal Ironworks by the Village Blacksmith," and how it appears on a product can be trademarked. Mary Hunt, publisher of *Cheapskate Monthly,* obtained a trademark on her newsletter name, when used in connection with the newsletter subject of frugality. (And once you apply, you are protected from the date of application.) However, ideas and short phrases can't be copyrighted or protected under the Trademark Laws. Barbara Brabec, author of *Homemade Money,* makes a clear distinction:

"The *artwork* on a can of cola can be *copyrighted.* The *name*—and the way it is expressed on that can—can be *trademarked.* The *formula* for the cola itself can be *patented.*"[4]

As the Culps found, a trademark can cost $200 or more, and take from several months to two years to obtain. Here's how to apply to register your trademark:.

- Contact the U.S. Copyright Office for *Trademarks* (Circular R13) or *Making It Legal,* or the Superintendent of Documents for booklet *General Informa*tion Concerning Trademarks, (free)

Seeking a Trademark

- Contact the Patent and Trademark Office for free information on how to obtain patents and trademarks.

- Do some preliminary trademark searching in the annually published *Trademark Register of the U.S.* (available at most large libraries), or

- You can do your own trademark search through Compuserve Information Service or another online service. Compuserve's TRADEMARKSCAN offers six trademark databases including three for North American trademark searches. Databases cover European and International trademarks. For example, the U.S. Federal database contains over 1 million records representing all active trademark registrations and pending applications filed with the U.S. Patent and Trademark Office (USPTO).

- First zero in on the trademark or brand name you want to use; do research at the library or online search of trademarks to make sure you aren't duplicating a registered trademark; then start using the trademark on your product or newsletter. Once you are using the trademark, you can apply for registration.

Working As a Team

Part of the success of Aircraft and Industrial Services, Inc. and Orna-Metal Ironworks is the teamwork between Margaret and Floyd. Both are enthusiastic hard workers who use their talents for the benefit of the enterprise. Although Floyd has the expertise in aircraft and mechanical design and engineering, Margaret is an integral part of the business. She helps in the metal shop, can operate the equipment, makes deliveries, and develops new products.

Floyd manages their metal shop which is filled with equipment, such as a large shear to cut the 4' by 12' sheets of metal into the required sizes for brackets or industrial parts, three punch presses, which put the proper sized holes in the metal, and a lathe, which shapes the steel into the right form. They also have a selection of grinders and sanders.

Together the Culps do their own bookeeping on a "Quickens" program on computer. They send their CPA the monthly payroll and he advises them what to hold out for Social Security, unemploy-ment, and taxes.

"People shudder when you talk about CPA's," says Floyd, "but he's a bargain." He adds that the "dig it out of a shoebox" method of bookkeeping that many home business owners use costs them time, money (especially if they aren't aware of the tax deductions available), and becomes stressful. "The first thing to do when starting your business is to find a good CPA!"

Best Advice on Pursuing Government Contracts

You'll need assistance on proper packaging that meets certain specifications and how to bid on government jobs. "Not knowing who to contact was a tough problem on the first government contract," Culp says. But they called the Bid Assistance Center at Rose State College and found immediate help. The director there said to come over and he did all he could to help them get the contracts.

Floyd and Margaret got in the van and drove the two hours to Oklahoma City where they spent an hour with her in the conference room. When they walked out, they knew everything they needed to know about military packaging, had all the specifications written out, and the pieces of the puzzle came together. "That kind of help is out there; you just need to know where to find it," says Floyd.

Call and visit:

Vocational-Technical schools and centers in your area, Small Business Assistance Centers, the Corps of Engineers, and Home-Based Business Associations. Every government base has a person who is assigned to small business. This consultant's full-time job is to help small business owners get government contracts, because a certain percentage have to be awarded to small businesses.

"If you are a small-business person, and can paint, or put hinges on doors, or make a part or product they are looking for, call and bid on the job. They need our help," adds Floyd.

Look for used equipment to save money and lower your

overhead. "We've bought all our equipment at auctions, going-out-of-business sales, including our first computer and software."

If layoff's seem possible or inevitable in your present employment, or if you see business is cutting back, start preparing to get out on your own. He advises, "Start thinking about what you want to do *while you still have income.* Begin building knowledge and tools, so that you have whatever you need to be on your way to a new business when or if layoff happens. It's rough to start out with no income and no direction."

Floyd, who was active in the local home-based business chapter for four years, serves as the President of the state-wide Home-Based Business Association, with the hope of encouraging others to pursue their dreams and develop their skills—and to equip those who are interested with the resources and knowledge that he was given which led to his highly successful Aircraft and Industrial Services, Inc.

The Culps are believers in "giving back" to their community and even to the next generation of Americans. "I don't really need to work this hard, but my generation is responsible to a great extent for the economic mess our country is in. I have some comfort to say I'm helping to fix this problem we created and not dump it on our grandkids," he says.

The United States government is the world's largest buyer of goods and services, with purchases by military and civilian facilities amounting to approximately $180 billion a year, ranging from airplane parts, cancer research, to paperclips. The government buys nearly every single category of service and product available.

Contracting With the Government

The U.S. Small Business Administration (SBA) is charged with the responsibility of making sure that small businesses obtain a fair share of government contracts and subcontracts. The SBA Government Contracting Division has numerous programs to assist small businesses in bidding and getting government contracts:

- Prime Contracting and Subcontracting Assistance program
- Procurement Automated Source System
- Certificate of Competency program
- The Natural Resources Sales Assistance program

The government contracting specialist at the local SBA office can help you understand federal regulations and guide you through the process of obtaining contracts, including how to get through roadblocks. The SBA Government Contracting Division offers free information on:

Government buying methods

Government specifications

Materials allocation

Delivery

Supplier problems

Offeror's rights and obligations

Appeal procedures, termination and default actions

Size criteria, and much more information.

5

The Posy Collection

Defining Success

Posy Lough of Simsbury, Connecticut, grew up in a family that had no money to buy gifts, so she and other family members resorted to making them. For Posy, this led to developing her skills and creativity in making crafts and eventually evolved into a successful home business that produces historic counted cross-stitch kits to museums, educational crafts and toys for children, and Advent and Lenten calendars for families.

In her senior year of college, Posy fell in love . . . with wholesale marketing! it happened quite by accident. She wanted a college ring but could not afford the price. So she had the idea of making and selling decoupage plaques containing drawings of scenes from her college.

Since Posy did not want to sell the plaques door-to-door in the dorm, she approached the manager of the college bookstore (her first encounter with a wholesale buyer). She showed him the handmade plaques and convinced him that they would sell in his store. The buyer bought her entire lot at a wholesale price!

As a result of this significant though small "first sale," Posy was able to purchase her college ring. But even more important, this was the beginning of a lifelong fascination with wholesale marketing. Since then, Posy has met successfully with buyers of small shops and large ones, as well as mega-department stores like Macy's and Bloomingdale's of New York. Here are some lessons she has learned about meeting with a wholesale buyer:

Before Meeting With the Buyer

Scouting

Learn about the set-up and nature of the business of the wholesale buyer *before* any meeting. Posy studies the latest catalogs and visits the shop or store as a customer and investigates questions such as:

- What is the nature, quality and general price range of the merchandise?
- How much variety is there in the merchandise?
- Does the business focus on fads or on more standard products?
- Is there anything there which resembles my products?
- Are there any obvious gaps in the merchandise which I can fill, either with existing or new products?
- What are the characteristics of the customers?
- What marketing themes are evident?

  What is the name and telephone number of the buyer?

Having gained this information, you can better discuss your products with the buyer. For example, "Now this ornament might go well with your third floor floral print promotion," offers a specific idea for consideration.

Scheduling

Most buyers don't operate on a drop-in basis; an appointment is usually necessary. "When I call a buyer to set up an appointment, I am prepared to describe *briefly* what I have in mind. But my objective is to say only enough during the call to secure the appointment." Then begin focusing on preparations.

Fabricating

A sure-fire way to get a NO from a wholesale buyer is to come to the meeting with a less-than-finished sample product. "But I plan to include a really nice box," simply will not work, Posy says. The buyer is a busy person, and is interested only in what a fully finished product looks like. So always be sure to fabricate a sample *complete in every detail.*

When possible, Posy likes to make up several samples, perhaps in different colors and sizes, in hopes of leaving them behind for further consideration.

Pricing

For some home business merchandise, it may be difficult to establish a profitable wholesale price. But you must be prepared with a realistic proposal. From your scouting activity, you should have an idea of the general retail price range of merchandise similar to yours. Your price should be high enough to cover production costs and help you make a profit, but reasonable enough to attract customers and for the store to make a profit. With this preparation and approach to the wholesale buyer, you should be on your way to a new account.

How Do You Measure Success

Success is different things to different people: to some it's more money, being well-known in the business or professional community; and to others it's a shorter commute, more time with family and a better quality of life. How is Posy measuring her success? "I can be at my son Kyser's parent-teacher conferences," she says. She can also be home when he is ill, and home when he arrives from the bus ride after school. She can take a morning to be involved in the church or community activities she considers important.

Yet with her home business, Posy has extra income, a creative outlet while raising her son, plus the relationships that develop through her business and the satisfaction she feels from producing high-quality products that truly help families. Letters she has received from all over the U.S. and world from people who have bought her products attest to the value they provide, and that would be satisfaction enough! She also benefits from using her talents to count for something, and the "mental health" benefits of staying busy, productive, and meeting her goals while caring for a family.

Success is a matter of levels to Posy: "Today it might be a buyer returning my call because the caller may be difficult to reach." Tomorrow it may be on a radio broadcast that mentions her products and gives the address for ordering a catalog, or the satisfaction she felt in how beautiful the Norman Rockwell museum kit turned out. When she was a new mom at home, it was filling an order and all it took to manage her time and pull it together. And success was experienced on the days she got the "big accounts": United States Military Academy at West Point, New York; Biltmore Estate in Ashville, North Carolina: and Great Smokey Mountains National Park in Tennessee, for example.

A Family Endeavor

"Success" to Posy also includes the family benefits they have enjoyed. The Posy Collection has brought the Lough family closer by working together. Posy, with a background in hand crafts, leads the business with her ideas, research, and marketing skills. She makes contact with museum staffs and works closely with them for historical and architectural accuracy.

Husband Tom Lough, who has a full-time job with the LEGO Dacta education division of LEGO Systems, Inc., helps write the kits' historical sketches and handles much of the technology: photography, computer work and laser printing. Kyser, 12, helps in the business by packing materials, labelling, and assembling kits. Three designers, including Posy's sister, Ceil Humphreys of Orlando, Florida, sketch new designs. Eight needlework hobbyists stitch the prototype samplers and determine the amount of floss needed.

Stitching a Business Based on History and Needlecraft

The Posy Collection brings a bright historical twist to the traditional pasttime of needlework. And in the process, they provide hands-on heritage with the counted cross-stitch kits that are sold in gift shops at famous historical sites.

Because Posy and Tom both enjoy a keen interest in history, they find their research a pleasure.

Typically, one of the Posy needlework kits consists of a line drawing of the sampler designs on a 12 by 18 inch rectangle of fabric, ample hanks of the colored floss required, a tapestry needle and an instruction sheet describing where the colors of floss are to be stitched. The kit also includes an information sheet telling the significance and history of the symbols in the design and a color photograph of how the sampler should look when completed. The finished item becomes a family heirloom.

Hobby-Turned-Business

How did a hobby turn into a business for this former teacher? When Posy and Tom were both teaching school, they were forced to do something on the side to make ends meet. With the summers off and her entrepreneurial spirit, she came up with two terrific ideas to market. One of these was a large Christmas wreath she created that sold extremely well locally. She decided to make an appointment with buyers at Lord and Taylor's and Macy's in New York City. As a result, Macy's ordered the wreaths for the next season and Lord and Taylor ordered wreaths and the new products she created each year, for ten years.

When Posy needed help filling orders in the busy summer production season, she enlisted other teachers who needed extra money. Each year the volume of her business grew until twenty-two teachers were working for her; that was the summer she got pregnant and quit her teaching job to care for her baby son. Then she cut back on her large wreath production and decided to create a smaller and less expensive-to-ship ornament using historic locations on the East Coast.

"You can't steal second base with your foot still on first."
—Anonymous

Posy's first kit was a crosstitch replica of Monticello, the home of Thomas Jefferson, which was architecturally correct. Posy went on to create seven kits for Monticello, then designs for Colonial Williamsburg, Mt. Vernon, and other historical sites. Now with custom crosstitch kits for over 30 locations, including: Norman

Rockwell Museum Gift Shop, Old Sturbridge Village, United States Naval Academy, and Epcot Center. All kits are produced, filled with embroidery floss, and mailed from their home.

Secrets To Success

Perseverance has been a key to the success of the Posy Collection. "It took me over two years to get the Norman Rockwell account," says Posy. "Every other kit had been taken from one of his paintings, and I wanted to do something original. Our strength was doing samplers of the place and the person.

The Norman Rockwell Foundation was in the process of fund-raising for a new museum to be built beside the Victorian home on the Rockwell property. Posy's designs centered around the four buildings (the old and new museum and the studio and Victorian home) with Rockwell's quote worked in with his portfolio and painter's palette: "My life's work and my pleasure is to tell stories through pictures." But it took months of perseverance and patience in obtaining the account, working with the museum shop manager and developing the design. But the months of diligent work and perseverance have brought rewards; the Rockwell kit has proved to be an excellent seller.

"If you don't persevere, you don't get anywhere," says Posy. There is a fine line between being too forceful and rude, and persistent and polite. "You can't be wimpy either," she adds. Don't throw in the towel if you are met with obstacles. Quickly swallow the disappointment or rejection and continue. There will be many times you'll get a "NO" and the door will close, but if you keep trying, you'll succeed.

Niche Marketing

The Posy Collection's niche is selling to museums. "Mass-producers don't want to do what I'm doing (producing and selling 4,000 to 5,000 kits per year) and there are enough museums out there for me and plenty of people," says Posy. "I found my niche right under my nose in Charlottesville, Virginia." Look in your own backyard, she advises. Often people overlook what is right over or under them. Hospital gift shops for instance. Every hospital has a gift shop. You could create something for the person who wants a quick gift like:

- If you draw, ask the buyer what kind of cards people want in a pinch; if it's baby cards, then come up with something clever like "Congratulations on your baby born at Memorial Hospital!"
- With an inexpensive button machine you can make cute, colorful buttons on card stock: "Can you believe I'm in the hospital on Christmas?" or "It was a BOY born at Memorial Hospital."

Whatever you do, you could do it for a hospital gift shop: clever corsages to pin on a pillow or gown, hospital gift baskets. Talk to auxiliary ladies. See what's selling and what's needed.

Niche marketing means developing specialized products that focus on smaller target markets. Home-based business is generally very niche-oriented and can take advantage of the opportunities available for specialized products and services. For example, one home business produces a line of athletic greetings cards for joggers, skiers, and other athletes. Another makes ornaments and mementoes out of red Georgia clay to sell at tourist and other gift shops in their state.

Here's the lesson: because big business is becoming more attuned to niche markets, home-based business may have to look for even smaller niches.

Here are four ways to capitalize on niche markets:

1. Aim at a specific target. Describe your customer's need in detail.

2. Talk to your customers and make sure you are solving their individual problems.

*Finding
Your
Niche*

3. Verify your findings with information from a variety of sources.

4. Follow the ABCD Rule: **A**lways **B**e **C**ollecting **D**ata.

A niche marketer never rests, but stays in close direct contact with her customer.

Posy's long hours of effort developing new products, marketing, and networking are yielding a growing business, both because of the benefits and for the enjoyment she derives from it. As founder of the Posy Collection says, "Home business has a lot to do with what you love and have a passion about—not just for money. You can best find your business by finding what you love to do."

Learn, Learn, Learn

Another of Posy's secrets of success is to *learn from others.* In addition to reading great books and trade journals, Posy enjoys reading inspirational books, including biographies and autobiographies of outstanding people who have made not only career success but contributed to the world around them. She also has studied texts for business courses, (she once read every book assigned at the Darden's School of Business) and recommends reading professional magazines in your area of interest. In addition, take advantage of every opportunity from people you do business with, especially the buyers you present products to.

For instance, in creating a design for Monticello, Posy planned to use the mansion as her focus. But in conferring with the buyer, she learned the pineapple design had been discovered in a recent excavation on the property. The buyer felt the pineapple design, a symbol for hospitality, had a much broader appeal than the Jefferson mansion. Posy incorporated that design as the focus of the crosstitch kit for the museum shop. The new kit has been a great seller.

It's a Buyer's Market (How to Make the Most Out of Your Appointment)

Be On Time

Buyers are extremely busy people who must make purchasing decisions which directly affect the success or failure of their businesses. They have no time to waste. So be on time for all your appointments and you'll start on a positive note! (In fact, aim to arrive *early* so you can look the store over once more)

Be Yourself

Although buyers are used to dealing with experienced representatives of large companies, they respect the small business person. Relax and act professional, but retain your natural personality and let the buyer get to know you.

Be a Student

Learn all you can about his buying methods, annual schedule, and when purchasing decisions are made for certain seasons. Don't be afraid to ask questions about terms or procedures that are new to you. And most of all, try to learn what the buyer needs.

Be ready to make the most of "yes" or "no": If the buyer says *yes* and places an order, agree on a shipping date, shipping procedures, and the prices. If possible, obtain a copy of a signed purchase order. If the buyer says *no,* realize that he or she is not rejecting you; try not to take it personally. Whatever you were offering did not fit their company's needs at that time. Remember that every "No" brings you closer to your next "Yes" if you listen and learn.

After the meeting, write down any feedback you gained from the buyer such as suggestions for future products or comments about packaging. Then follow up by:

- Staying in regular contact with the buyer by telephone and through the mail. Send a thank you note and include your business card. Send a sample of a new product you develop and follow up a few days later with a phone call.
- If the buyer placed an order, call once or twice before the delivery date with assurance of the order being on schedule. If you did not get an immediate order, but the buyer requested a sample or photograph of the product in a different color or style, send what is requested as soon as possible.
- If the appointment did not result in an order, evaluate your feedback from the buyer. Consider his objections and how

you could change your product to overcome these. Brainstorm on what other businesses which might be interested. And finally, stay in touch with the buyer and be open to future needs and possibilities. As Posy says, "Determination is the key to long-term success!"

Do-It-Yourself PR

Another key for the home-based entrepreneur is learning how to generate free publicity for your business. Since small businesses usually have little or no budget for advertising, one of the best ways to "do-your-own PR" is to write and send Press Releases.

As Posy says, "You've got to keep the name of your business in front of people." Sending Press Releases can get you feature articles in the business section, or even on the front page of the local or regional newspaper.

Send out press releases often: when you introduce a new product, when you attend a conference or trade show, when you speak at a seminar, expand your enterprise, or contribute in some way to your community through offering your service to benefit a charity or auction or displaying your products at an elementary school. Newspaper stories increase your visibility and credibility, and are great free advertising for your business. Here's how to:

Prepare Winning Press Releases

- If you are writing your own Press Release, find some models of press releases and let them guide your format. In addition to these suggestions, see the books in the Resource Box for samples. If you have a friend in the newspaper or advertising business experienced in composing press releases, enlist his or her assistance in writing your first one.
- Type the entire press release on one page, front only—and preferably a one-page press release. Editors are busy and don't have time to read a long news story.
- Type "For Immediate Release" at the top of the page.
- Double space lines of the press release.

- Send an original of your press release, not a xeroxed copy.
- Cover the **who, what, when, where, and how**, and make sure your facts, dates, and figures are straight.
- Have good black and white publicity photos on hand.
- Time your mailing: Some PR veterans say that mailing your press release on a Friday is advantageous because it arrives on the editors' desk on Monday or Tuesday, when they're not as busy with deadlines as later in the week.
- Follow up. A few days after sending your news release, call and ask:"Have you received my press release? Do you think you can use it?" Offer to be interviewed or supply photos and other information. And don't forget to thank the editor for his consideration and time. Be persistent but not demanding, warmly businesslike instead of obnoxious.
- Always be sure to include where readers can contact you: your business address, phone and fax number, and/or e-mail address so that it will be included in any article or story that mentions your business.
- At the close of your press release, skip a line, center and type three # (pound) signs with a space between each one (# # #), or "-30-" to indicate the end.

Resources For Generating Your Own Free Publicity

Here are Posy's personal favorites, that contain many practical ideas on PR for the home business entrepreneur. To save money, check your local library both in the business section (658's) and "New Non-fiction Books" section and study the book to get at least one or two new ideas on publicity to put into practice. One of the books may have so much valuable advice, you'll want to have it on your shelf.

Guerrilla PR, Michael Levine
(NY: Harper-Collins, 1993)
Guerrilla Marketing Handbook, Jay Levinson
(NY: Houghton-Mifflin, 1994)

HOME BUSINESS HAPPINESS
The Posy Collection

Do-It-Yourself Publicity, David Ramacitti
(NY: AMACOM, 1990)

Do-It-Yourself Advertising, David Ramacitti
(NY: AMACOM, 1992)

Do-It-Yourself Marketing, David Ramacitti
(NY: AMACOM, 1994)

Home Business Ideas

Christmas Decorations: Make quality holiday decorations for the entire home or office. Make decorations from fabric, wood, or your favorite rts and crafts medium. Sell them to Christmas stores, businesses, gift or specialty stores, or through mail order.

Local Color Greeting Cards: Design a line of greeting cards depicting your city or local points of interest. Use your favor ite art form: stencils, photography, or pen-and-ink or watercolor drawings (yours, your friend's, or even your child's)

Market the "local color" cards as Posy does. Sell "Connecticut Country Christmas" cards wholesale to local gift shops, or sell "San Francisco Scenes" to travel center and gift shops.

Toys: There is a huge market for toys. Try making them from fabric or from wood. Make them movable, educational, or huggable. Test them on kids you know and love, and be sure to meet safety standards.

T-shirts and Night-Shirts: Use your skills to create wearable, contemporary art, "local color" landmark T-shirts, or shirts with a message. Sell to specialty or clothing shops, catalog companies, or wholesale buyers. Design T-shirts for the local high school special events or sports teams.

For a free "Posy Collection" catalog, or more information send a self-addressed stamped envelope to:

Posy Collection
20 Whitcomb Dr.
Simsbury, CT 06070

6

From Small Beginnings To Phenomenal Growth

The Family Network, Inc. Adoption Agency

Luke Leonard and his wife, Georgia, both with master's degrees in social work, served in a large hospital in St. Louis in the late 1970's. Georgia, a R.N. and M.W.W., worked as a nurse, and Luke, a social worker and counselor. Although they enjoyed their work at the hospital, they wanted to invest their lives from a vocational direction to something that would bring meaning and purpose.

When they adopted their daughter, "Asha" (meaning "hope") from India, their career direction began to be clarified. Luke and Georgia came from large families (each is one of 10 children), and they uphold a strong sense of community-service and belief in the institution of adoption. Therefore, they committed themselves to child welfare work by opening an adoption agency, "Family Adoption and Counseling Services, Inc." in their Missouri home in 1979. After two years in their home office, they moved to a small office and later a larger one.

As with all non-profit, IRS-approved, tax-exempt entities, their adoption agency had a board of directors and they were paid a salary that was determined by the board. Although every state has different requirements for an adoption agency to be licensed, holding master's degrees in social work with a certain number of years' experience in the child welfare field and having the agency located in a separate office are common requirements in all states.

Luke is the Executive Director of the agency, and Georgia is the Assistant Executive Director and Director of Foreign Adoptions. Luke now operates out of a small office, whereas Georgia works out of their home while caring for their six children, ages twelve to eighteen.

Since they are parents of three adopted children from India, Guatemala, and Bangladesh, one domestic adopted biracial son (and two biological daughters), the Leonards have special empathy for adoptive parents. In addition, their experience in counseling and child welfare equips them to provide support and help for these families.

In the past 15 years that the Leonards have been operating their agency, they have placed over one thousand children from all over the world. They have also opened an orphanage in Guatemala City, Guatemala, and do many foreign as well as domestic, adoptions.

Expansion And Growth

In 1990 the Leonards decided to take another step of growth by becoming certified in the state of Illinois and eight counties in northern California (a state said to rarely gives state-wide certification to any agency; the Leonards are licensed from San Francisco to Monterey), moving their family to California to establish their office there. In that same year, the agency changed its name to "The Family Network, Inc." to more accurately reflect its growing dimension of total family-focused care on a national and international basis.

Family Network currently has adoption programs in China, Russia, India, Moldova in Eastern Europe, Honduras, Guatemala, and Columbia. The goal of Family Network's domestic adoption program is to offer a loving alternative for expectant mothers and build a bridge between children and adoptive parents. Their mission is clear: quality personal service based on a respect for life orientation. They believe in an inter-generational approach to family concerns coupled with a linkage to appropriate community resource service through its many programs:

- Free Pregnancy Counseling
- Adoption Home Studies
- Counseling with Adoptive Parents
- Child Placement Supervision
- Necessary Court Work
- Interstate Compact Coordination
- Networking and Coordination with Community Services
- Coordination with Immigration and Naturalization

The Family Network, Inc. is helping over one thousand people per year and placing many needy children from third world countries into loving, permanent homes.

The more clearly you can define your mission, the more focused, motivated, and successful you will be in meeting your goals. In addition, you will reduce frustration and help you make better day-to-day decisions. Here's three ways to begin:

> *What Is Your Mission and Purpose? One Of the Best Ways to Focus Your Home Business and Your Life Is to Write a Mission Statement.*

1. *Identify your gifts and talents.* At what are you best? What do you really enjoy doing because you do it so well?
2. *Review your experiences.* Ask "What have I learned so far?" (Our greatest lessons often come through difficult times, and even pain. Factor these into your life purpose.)
3. *Decide what is really important,* so when the tyranny of the urgent knocks at your door, or when your priorities get out of whack, you'll know how to handle it.[5]

Requirements, Costs, And Legalities Of International And Domestic Adoption

The need for international adoption services is great. It is estimated that, internationally, there are ten million children—in India, China, Guatemala, and other third-world countries—who are orphaned and have nowhere to go. In the orphanage in Guatemala where Georgia goes two or three times a year, most are abandoned children from the hospital. Some are eventually reclaimed by a parent, and the majority are adopted into American homes. There are also a vast number of orphaned children available for adoption in Africa, Romania, and Russia. These countries do not have welfare agencies like our United States Department of Human Services, so the children are sent to orphanages, often receiving poor care because of lack of funds.

Moreover, the upper classes in these countries don't often adopt; there are no middle-class families; and the lower-class parents lack the money and resources to take another child in and can barely care for their own biological children. Since the country cannot take proper care of its children, it allows the children to be adopted in homes in America and Western Europe.

With the cost of foreign adoptions extremely expensive. An average international adoption costs from $10,000 to $20,000, including agency and legal fees, home study, airline tickets, etc. Domestic adoptions run from $10,000 up for a private adoption and much less for a state adoption through a public welfare agency for an older, disabled or minority child, and $5,000–6,000 for a healthy child. The Leonards hope to provide more aid for birth mothers and scholarships for families who are worthy and desire to adopt a child but can't afford it. They want to do more pro-adoptive advertising to reach more families and birth mothers.

"The U.S. media is more anti-adoption than pro-adoption. That hurts the adoption process," says Luke. "There are many more positive than negative stories, but the media highlights the negative stories." The Leonards believe there needs to be more education on the beauty of adoption because, if birth mothers understood the joys and positive aspects of adoption, they would not abort their babies or keep them when it is not appropriate. Thus, the 21 percent of American couples who are infertile and want to adopt a child could have a chance to do so.

Advertising: How Does The Family Network, Inc. Let Parents Know About Their Adoption Services?

By having ads in several national adoption publications and being listed in the Yellow Pages of the phone book in primary cities in the three states in which they are licensed, prospective clients find out about their adoption services. In addition, church groups, pastors, counselors and physicians refer families to them. Word-of-mouth from parent-to-parent is often one of the best means by which information about their adoption services has spread.

The Leonards also give presentations to Adoption Support Groups for Parents and speak at regional and national education meetings on adoption. Their 800 number enables people seeking adoption assistance to contact the agency from anywhere in the U.S.

Best Advice For Those Interested In The Adoption Field

First, seek assistance from others experienced in the field of child welfare and adoption. From the very beginning, invest in the services and counsel of a good attorney and certified public accountant. Using their professional services will save you much stress, money, and many legal difficulties. After gaining the necessary degrees (which includes an undergraduate degree and Masters in Social Work), work in the child welfare field to gain experience. Research the additional certification requirements in your particular state.

Adoptive Families of America,
3333 Highway 100 North;
Minneapolis, MN 55422 (Phone
612-535-4829) Excellent vehicle for
informing parents of adoption
resources and support groups for
adoptive parents.

Publications In the Field of Adoption

International Concerns Committee for Children,
Boulder, CO (303-494-8333)

Why Was I Adopted?
A book for children; illustrated; large print paperback,
NY: Livingstone, Carroll Publishing Group.

Handling "On Call" And Finding A Balance In Life

How do the Leonards divide responsibilities and balance home, children, and adoption agency? Like an OB-Gyn doctor who delivers babies at all hours, Luke is helping to "deliver babies" to adoptive families and has to always be available and on call.

Dividing responsibilities and their "co-parenting style," is one way the Leonards balance their time between home and work. Although Luke is primarily responsible for The Family Network's marketing, finances and direct services to parents, such as home studies for adoption, he also is very involved with their own children and helps keep the household running. He makes meals, does dishes, and coordinates the children's activities if Georgia has a client on the phone during the supper hour. Sometimes when emergencies develop or when Georgia is working with people in a foreign country eight or nine hours ahead of the U.S. time and the call comes at a "prime time," it is necessary for Luke to take over.

Georgia, as Assistant Executive Director and Director of Foreign Adoptions, does a lot of in-home phone work, international coordinating of adoptions, and correspondence. She does the primary parenting of their children and has a volunteer part-time secretary to help with agency work. "We've found husbands and wives can work together effectively if each has his or her *own area* of efficiency and authority.

With six children and a full schedule, the Leonard children have learned to be flexible. "We've learned to be sensitive to their needs, and they have learned to pitch in," Luke says. "Sometimes it is good for them to adjust and wait, but sometime their needs come first."

Each of their children have a chore to be completed daily such as vacuuming, laundry folding, washing dishes. In the business, they help address envelopes, help with picnics and entertain the little children, escort children from other countries, help with translations from Spanish, and act as receptionist when mom is not available.

One of the benefits they already see is how "in touch" their children are with what their parents do for work. "Most parents leave, and their children have no idea what their parents really do at their jobs," he adds. "Our kids talk about what we do. They've been to the orphanage in Guatemala and even helped take care of the children. When Erin was asked on a college application what her parents do, she was able to describe it in full detail.

How to Avoid Creating A Monster When Working With Your Spouse

- Listen to each person's opinion
- Make sure each person knows for certain that he/she is of value as a person to the business
- Make sure each person profits when the business is doing well financially
- Be flexible with schedules so each person's needs are allotted for as much as possible
- Create a savings immediately, so that you will have the resources to purchase the necessary time-saving equipment and hire competent staff to enable better control of your enterprise. Learn to delegate and realize no one is indispensable!

Avoiding Burnout

"The best advice I can give is to decide your priorities based on a twenty-year outcome," says Georgia. Ask yourself: "What will I wish I had done in this situation twenty years from now? If I consistently allow work to be the priority, will my children resent me? Is the added income worth it?"

Because her work is flexible, Georgia can adjust it to the needs of her family except at times when everything seems to be happening at once. "I see myself as a mother first, and Director of Foreign Adoptions second," she adds. Burnout is a always a possibility with any family or home business.

- When burnout seems to be developing, sometimes the work that is not *now* can be put in a closet or room where it can't be seen for a few days.

"Burnout Busters"

- Shorten work hours temporarily to allow recovery time.
- Engage in a fun, silly or meaninglessness activity for an evening
- Treat yourself to a Saturday or Sunday morning breakfast in bed and read until noon. Take a long walk by the ocean or in a garden.

And for good mental health, do only *one* thing at a time. For example, when showering, savor the warm water on your head, shoulders, etc. When driving, savor the vibration of your feet on the floor of the car. When eating, savor each fork full.

Become aware of your body signs, advises Luke. Stress in your vocalizations, temperament elevation, irritability, fatigue: all signs that burnout is taking its toll and a break is needed. Learn to have fun and relax, knowing that it is healthy and necessary.

The Family Network, Inc. is good evidence that it is possible to integrate family and business with integrity and still enjoy one's children, spouse, and career. In the Leonard's case, not only their family benefits from the success of their mission, but also thousands of children and families in the U.S. and around the world.

The Family Network, Inc.
284 Foam Street, #103
Monterey, California 93940
(800) 888-0242

7

Never Give Up: Believe In What You Do!

Mother & Daughter Originals Gift Baskets

Five years ago Peggy Jones, although employed full-time, wanted to start a small business. She and her husband travelled to California to visit three couples who shared an interest in glider airplane models. One of the couples had come from Australia to travel in the U.S., so Peggy decided to take each couple a Texas gift basket. The problem was she couldn't find one and most general gift baskets were $40–45 a piece.

Since Peggy had always given practical gifts in creative containers, like a colander with kitchen tools for a bride-to-be, or a trash can with practical gifts inside for a graduate, she bought cookbooks, queso and other Texas food items. The Texas gift baskets went over so well that Peggy began to look at baskets in California.

Back at home, she talked to her daughter, Melinda, about the idea and they gathered information, products, baskets, and supplies. They experimented, looked around to see where they were going to sell the gift baskets, and tried a few different avenues.

The first market they tried was the craft mall. Craft malls were just opening in the Dallas area and becoming popular. They rented space in three craft mall booths to display the baskets. But people stole items out of the baskets and rewrapped other items, so their experience in craft malls was short-lived.

They also joined the Dallas Chamber of Commerce for the connections and networking. At events, such as the Chamber's "Business After Hours" group of 500–800 people, they could exhibit their baskets for an additional charge. This networking event resulted in several new accounts.

They also advertised "Mother and Daughter Originals" gift baskets in the Yellow Pages in the surrounding suburbs of Plano, Carrollton, Garland, and the Dallas metroplex area. Peggy lived in Garland, where the zoning restrictions specified—no employees can be hired to work in your home business, no advertising or signs at your home, and no customers coming to your home to purchase your products. Not one to be daunted, Peggy says, "We set up appointments and took samples to show prospective customers."

The business grew, while Peggy was still working full-time during the first year of the business. "Although it was really difficult time-wise," she says, "This was a great learning time and I did all I could to learn the business."

She took floral design classes to learn how to use silk and other flowers. She and Melinda attended "The Jubilees" in Florida, a conference and trade show for the gift basket business. The Jubilees included three days of classes in the basics of making gift baskets, marketing, mega-orders, using balloons in basketry, and everything else connected with gift baskets. (See Sidebar for information)

It was a great opportunitity to observe and learn from top basket makers because the conference also included a competition of more than 5,000 gift basket entries from all over the world.

Starting A Gift Basket Business

A gift basket business is good because start-up costs are relatively low compared to other small businesses. Materials and supplies can cost up to $500 for baskets, ribbons, and small gift items, plus advertising (in the Yellow Pages, as Peggy Jones did, business cards, and brochure with pricing) and other expenses.

Besides the demand for individual gift baskets, corporations and businesses are also great customers. Businesses order baskets for conventions, special occasions, thank you gifts for employees and big accounts, and Christmas gifts for employees.

Finding wholesale suppliers for gourmet foods, decorative items, flowers, and small gifts will lower the cost of the contents of your completed baskets. To find wholesale suppliers, Peggy goes to regional gift and trade shows, subscribes to industry publications, and attends seminars such as **Jubilees**.

For information on Jubilees contact:

> Festivities Publications, Inc.
> 1205 West Forsyth Street
> Jacksoville, FL 32204
> (904) 634-1902

Besides publishing *Gift Basket Review*, they also publish a magazine for the floral industry and balloonists.

Secrets Of Success

Peggy attributes her success to a never-give-up attitude. She loves what she does, is willing to work hard, and her watchword is: "If you are going to be successful never give up, and believe in yourself."

"I enjoy coming to work every day and that's part of it, getting in there and getting everything done, because all businesses have parts that aren't fun—like everything done, because all businesses have parts that lots of paperwork," she says. Peggy would rather be putting creative baskets together and looking through catalogs for new ideas. "But without keeping up with paperwork and bookkeeping, there wouldn't be any business!"

She also attributes part of her success to her business experience. She was in the lumber and hardware business for six years, and the rest of her working life was an executive secretary. One of her assets is coordinating tasks and communication between departments, an administrative talent which comes in handy in any business.

"People don't realize how hard you have to work to make a go of a business. You've got to put your whole soul into it," she says. "You won't get rich overnight, so you have to really like what you're doing or you'll get burned out on it."

For the first three years, Peggy's home was the location of "Mother and Daughter Originals." Working out of her home cut down on overhead and thus her pricing, but she didn't have the exposure she needed. Two years ago, Peggy purchased a gift basket shop in Dallas, moving from her home-based enterprise to a store front location for "Mother and Daughter Originals." When asked what is the best time to move from home-based into a store front, Peggy said, "When you get to the point where it's impossible to grow."

"There came a time for me when people wanted to see baskets, and I just couldn't have large amounts of traffic in my home." Also, her city had zoning laws that didn't work for home-based businesses. Her gift basket business now has greater visibility and walk-in traffic. Normally she has part-time help in her shop for at least four hours a day, and hired another part-time employee who does marketing for her. "This part-time help is very valuable as there are so many things I need to be here for, quoting for large jobs, working with customers. My marketing person networks at meetings and follows up with customers."

Peggy also teaches an adult continuing education course on gift-basket basics, which includes the mechanics, themes, and strategies of building baskets that sell and please customers. She also teaches advanced gift basket design. She passes on what she has learned to help others beginning in the business be successful.

"Mother & Daughter Originals" carries: Texas Baskets, Gourmet Baskets, Fruit Baskets, Corporate Gifts, Centerpieces, Conventions, Company Meetings, Family Reunions, Bridal Parties, and Fundraisers. They also create special baskets from their selection of products, baskets, and unique containers for every occasion or event. The full-color brochure which includes a price list, 800 ordering phone number, address, local number, and other information is an essential part of her marketing and advertising.

- Stick to a theme, such as Cajun or Victorian, or to items related to one food, such as chocolate or coffee

- Don't mix fragrance and foods. The food will absorb the fragrance

Basket Basics

- Arrange and anchor items securely so they don't get jumbled in delivery

Gift-Basket Tip: Always Give Good Service and Sell Quality Products.

For Mother's Day, for instance, she loves a Victorian theme. The Victorian baskets have a cup and saucer, teas or gourmet coffees, a box of special cookies, a feather fan, lace doilies or embroidered napkin. They do a colorful, personalized basket in which one side is made up of the recipient's favorite flowers in silk, and the other side is fruit.

Four Top Ways To Succeed In The Gift Basket Business

1. *Before beginning, contact your city, county and state health departments for all regulations you need to abide.* In many states, you must go through a food handlers course if your gift baskets contain certain kinds of food, or if you touch or wrap the food. If you make any of the food, you must have a commercial kitchen that has been approved by the health department.

   Although "Mother and Daughter Originals carries a big variety of food in their gift baskets, from chocolates to gourmet coffees and teas, Texas Caviar to "Mean Green Salsa" all of their food is already individually wrapped products; they don't prepare or touch the food.

   She also does not carry food unless it has been produced in a commercial kitchen registered in the state of Texas. "Otherwise, it would be a liability for me." She advises that you must follow liquor laws, and all other state regulations. Mother & Daughter Originals packs only non-alcoholic beverages in their baskets, so they did not have to apply for a liquor license or deal with the shipping regulations, etc.

2. *Contact your state's Department of Agriculture.* The Department of Agriculture can be a great benefit and supporter of your business. Mother & Daughter Originals belongs to the Texas Department of Agriculture "Taste of Texas" Program. The program lists Mother and Daughter Originals in their advertising and brochures, keeps her abreast of new products and all the different food shows to attend and exhibit baskets. "Not many gift basket businesses belong to the Agriculture program, but it's been a tremendous benefit and great advertising," she says.

The Department of Agriculture also sends her a list of all members that make a certain product in Texas—for instance, salsa. "This saves me a lot of time in tracking down items and gives me permits on buying in quantities."

3. *Carry quality products.* The pitfall many gift basket businesses fall into is they try to skimp on products and it really shows. Peggy never puts anything in her baskets without tasting or trying them. Cookies, for example, can have beautiful packaging, be very expensive, but not taste good. "I look for quality in the product, then how it's packaged, and how many cases you have to buy."

You have to look at minimums, Peggy adds, especially in a small business. Every company has a minimum amount you must buy.

4. *Be competitive in your pricing.* If you are going into the gift basket business, know:
- Who are your competitors?
- What products they are selling?
- How are they priced?

It makes a big difference whether you are paying rent or not and what your overhead is. "I could price the baskets lower when I was operating out of my home, but when I moved into a retail location I had a higher overhead." It's difficult if you have a lot of customers and you raise your prices $5.00 each. It's best to sell your baskets at a price the market will bear, be competitive, and sell a *quality product.*

The best price is one that will maximize the *profits* from your business, and profit depends on costs, selling price, and the number of items you sell.

Your price should:
- Be high enough to cover all production and marketing costs.
- Help you make a profit.
- Be reasonable and competitive enough to attract customers.
- Build sales volume.

Pricing Your Products

You should consider these elements that contribute to price:
1. *Direct costs:* Raw materials + Labor (Production time)
2. *Overhead costs:*
   Production: Tools, equipment, depreciation + Workshop/ Studio Maintenance and Utilities
   Non-production: Marketing and storage + Special fees, insurance, taxes, Bookkeeping
3. *Profit for investment, savings, future business expansion:* The basic formula for pricing is simple. The sum of the above costs over a certain period of time (day, week, month, year) divided by the number of items produced equals the selling price of each item, or the unit price.[6]

Peggy also advises subscribing to *Gift Basket Review,* one of the publications for the industry, which helped her find suppliers and gain valuable marketing information. (See address/phone # for Festivities Publications, Inc.)

More Resources for the Gift Basket Business:
The Gift Basket Gazette
9655 Chimney Hill Lane, Suite 1036
Dallas, Texas 75243

Great Ideas for Gift Baskets, Bags, & Boxes, Kathy Lamancusa,
 Filled with many gift design ideas from beginner to advanced levels
(order from *Gift Basket Gazette,* address above)
The Perfect Basket, Diane Phillips (NY: Hearst Books, 1994)
How to Start Your Own Gift Basket Business, Bruce Webster,
Income Opportunities Manuals, P. O. Box 40
Vernon, NJ 07462

Gift Basket Businesses Flourish In Small Towns

Small towns are an ideal place for gift basket businesses because there is often little available in the way of specialty products and gifts, whereas the gift basket business is more competitive in large cities across the country. Products for baskets can be ordered by catalog and delivered by UPS, so a wide range of gift items is available for creating baskets that sell.

Pitfalls Of The Gift Basket Business

Peggy believes in telling people the good, bad and the ugly, including the pitfalls of the gift basket business so that you can proceed realistically and even anticipate or prevent problems:

Long hours: The hours are long, especially at holidays such as Valentine's Day, Christmas, Mother's Day, Secretaries' Day. "My children are all grown," says Peggy, "and my husband is supportive." For the first few years, she worked seven days a week, so all her weekends were tied up with the gift basket business. "You really have to love it! At Christmas holidays, it's around the clock; Mother's Day is our second largest holiday. Thanksgiving is quite busy."

Planning and buying ahead: You have to plan months ahead to prepare for your holiday rush business. In June prior to the Christmas season, for example, you have to start your buying for products.

Having enough capital: Being aware of all the expenses involved and having enough capital to cover them is vital. Many gift basket beginners miss the hidden costs, which can be overwhelming. If you're in a retail space, you must have insurance coverage that includes liability. You also must have a good-sized inventory which takes solid capital.

Being up front and legal by following all the city planning and zoning regulations and applying for a sales tax number. "This is a big pitfall," says Peggy. "Many people just skip this part or think it is too complicated. You must apply under your business name through your county tax office or State comptroller's office, be registered, and report and pay sales tax to the state in which you live and do business. Check with your CPA and/or attorney and make a list of the bases you'll need to cover legally.

To carry live plants or flowers in your baskets, you must have a permit and be registered through the Department of Agriculture for a fee of approximately $60 a year. An inspector comes out to your house or business space and inspects plants, dish gardens, etc.

"I feel better being up-front and knowing what I'm supposed to be doing, rather than having someone come in and shut me down," she says. "Doing business honestly and legally saves a lot of heart ache."

When the *Dallas Morning News* wrote and carried a feature article about "Mothers & Daughters Originals," the story ran in newspapers in St. Louis, Las Vegas, Hartford, Connecticut and other places around the country, which resulted in good exposure to the national market. As the business continues to grow, Peggy is grateful for all the opportunities, for the adventure and creativity the business offers, and the chance to help others start a business they love.

For more information contact:

> Mother & Daughter Originals:
> Gift Baskets for All Occasions,
> 2828 Centerville Road, Suite 105,
> Dallas, Texas 75228
> (800) 995-5499.

8

Cash With Your Computer

Desktop Publishing And Word Processing

Desk-top publishing is one of the most profitable of in-home businesses. Writing services are needed more than ever by a variety of businesses and organizations, because companies are down-sizing their in-house office staffs and sending out more and more of their word-processing and desk-top publishing to freelancers. That produces opportunitites for industrious people like Ross Tunnell who have writing skills, a word processor, and the versatility to pursue different avenues of work.

Ross Tunnell of Gresham, Oregon, had his first experience with computers with a Vic-20 in the early 1980's. The Vic was little more than keyboard with memory, using the family TV as its monitor. Their children spent hours pouring over computer magazines and copying down programs they could type into the computer. Eventually they got a cassette tape recorder rigged to back up the programs they had typed in. Up to that time, every time they turned off the computer, they lost everything.

Recently, their son Matthew, now a systems' analyst and computer guru at a big corporation, said, "Essentially, everything I do at work I learned on the Vic-20. The concepts were all there."

Making Cash With Computers

The next step in their computer acquisition was an IBM PC in 1985. With such an expensive investment, Ross felt compelled to find ways to make money with it. Their first serious effort at computer entrepreneurship was to take out an ad in the *Writer's*

Digest magazine under the category, "We Type Manuscripts." They had registered a DBA (Doing Business As) Portland Clerical Services with the state and had opened an account at the bank.

"The first month we heard nothing," says Ross. "The second month there were a couple of inquiries." However, it was in the third month that there were enough responses to start making money.

How did they price their word processing services? Ross checked in the ad section of the magazine for the going rate per page, and then wrote or called other writers who had ads in for several months (which meant they were making enough money to keep running ads). They decided to position their rate at the lower end and charged $1.00 a page. Then they gradually raised the per page rate.

Over the next few years, their clients generated from that ad included a doctor in eastern Oregon who was writing a book on "The Primal Scream." Then there was a Romance novelist from Cape Cod who enlisted their services. They produced a newsletter for a political activist and a professor's critique on the works of William Shakespeare. After running the ad for about two years, they dropped it.

"Eight years later we still occasionally receive a letter of inquiry from someone who has seen one of our ads in an old issue," says Ross. "Mostly the inquiries come from prisoners." Apparently they have a lot of old *Writer's Digest* magazines lying around in prison libraries!

Ways To Make Money With Your Computer

Since those early days of word-processing, Ross has found other ways to make money on the computer. As he says, "The secret of success in a home business is finding something that people don't like to do and doing it for them—for pay." That's just what he did. Here are some of the ways to make money on your home computer:

1. *Heritage History*—You can help older people tell their story to their grandchildren and turn it into a self-published collection of history.

2. *Annual Reports*—You can write annual reports for small businesses or corporations, or help the church secretary get ready for the annual meeting.

3. *Counseling Center Newsletter*—Counselors are too busy to write articles for a newsletter that will keep them in touch with their clients, so you can do it for them. The newsletter is a great tool for expanding client base in the counseling field, so they would welcome your skills to produce one. Also most counselors have a book or two inside their heads that you can help get into print.

4. *Key in for Local Firms*— Let businesses know you can help with their times of overload. They appreciate your doing word-processing at home, because it keeps their computers free.

5. *Bulk Mailing*—Most businesses on occasion want to increase sales by mailing to their customers or mailing to prospective customers. Do it for them.

6. *Transcription*—Public speakers, preachers, and educators need their talks transcribed so they can publish articles, pamphlets and books. In addition, medical doctors need transcription of their appointments and patient histories for their files and records.

7. *Teach others*—After you have mastered a word-processing program like WordPerfect 6.1 or a new version of MicroSoft Word, offer to tutor others.

8. *Do layout and editing for publishing companies.* Frequently these days one or more of the editors for a publishing company is out-of-house, or even across the country from the home office. Also, many publishers use free-lance editors.

9. *Designing and producing brochures, catalogs, and flyers for businesses.* With all the great desktop publishing software available, this is a wide-open field for home-based businesses. Some home businesses are so busy

specializing just in this category and have little time left to do other tasks.

10. *Promotional writing,* such as writing and sending out press releases for individual authors or businesses is a hot field for the home-based computer specialist with writing talent.

11. *Do mailings for local businesses.* You can go to restaurants, ice cream stores, seminar speakers, doctors, and propose an inexpensive plan to increase their clients the restaurant owner offers a free dessert or meal weekly. The owner keeps a glass bowl out that customers put their business cards in and every week the drawing comes out of the pool of business cards. You offer to type a mailing list from the cards, and send out a mailing from the restaurant or business. "Word Perfect 5.1 or later has the best sorting utility; you can sort by 6 different variables and you don't even need a database to do it," says Ross. Use the "Mail Merge" function.

12. *Do overload work for word processing businesses, legal and medical transcriptionists.* Contact other word processing businesses that have been around longer than you have and let them know you are available if they are swamped and need help transcribing, typing reports, or anything they are typing.

13. *Resumé writing services*—writing and designing effective resumés and cover letters for people seeking employment or a change of career.

You *can* support your family or generate the income you need by developing a word-processing service, if you are willing to be versatile and flexible. Ross and his wife have supported themselves and their six children on the income from theirs. However, don't get stuck in thinking you can only write free-lance articles for magazines, or just type manuscripts and resumes. I can tell you from my experience as a freelance writer, that we must do many different kinds of projects and writing work to stay in business!

Consider your talents and skills and your equipment. Brainstorm about how you could apply these skills to the business world. *Diversify,*and watch your opportunities grow!

Adventures In Word Processing: Heritage History

Heritage History—or helping someone get their life story into print—was one of the "ways to make money computing" that Ross enjoyed the most. "I started out by contacting the social director of a upscale retirement center in our community," he says. He made sure it was a fairly nice facility because he needed a clientele who could pay for his services. Ross met with the activities coordinator and offered to speak at lunch on Heritage History. At the scheduled luncheon activity in the fall, he spoke of the benefits of preserving one's life stories. He also presented the idea that it would make a marvelous Christmas present to give each of their children, grandchildren, and great-grandchildren a copy of their life's story.

"There is a little of Laura Ingalls Wilder in all of us!" Ross adds. He got several clients from his initial presentation at the retirement center. One couple he worked with had come to Oregon in a wagon drawn by oxen. Most of their story they had handwritten, and they even had some pictures they wanted to include.

With the help of a local quick-print shop, he typed their "Heritage History," made Xerox copies of the pictures and placed them where they illustrated the stories. The pages were laid out 5-1/2 by 8 inches, which is a standard page folded in half. The local quick-print shop photocopied 35 copies and comb-bound them.

The elderly couple's children were very appreciative of the booklet. They showed it to their friends and word got around. In fact, so many people showed an interest in the booklet that they contacted a regular publisher and had it published for a much wider distribution. Ross had fortunately saved a copy of the booklet on a backup disk and was able to send the original version to the publisher on the computer disk. And if Ross had been a little more entrepreurial, he could have even made more income from the project by handling the full publication himself.

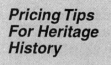

Pricing Tips For Heritage History

You can use these prices and packages as guides to developing your own. These are pricing guides. You can set two or three levels of Heritage History packages:

- *Deluxe:* 32 page booklet, plus a 20–30 minute audio cassette tape

- Writer does interviews, transcribing, composing, lay-out, cover, etc. for completed booklet at a total project price of $1500.

- *Economy:* 32 page booklet of your life history/family history from already existing handwritten or typewritten stories or notes that the writer inputs into the computer.

Writer does not conduct interviews, and does no research. $15.00 per hour (If the person's stories are difficult to read or you are working from difficult to hear cassette tapes, you may be able to do only 6 pages an hour, and the work is much slower. So charging by the hour may be more realistic.)

In any of the Heritage History booklets Ross undertook, he created a cover with graphics, and in some cases a photo cover (one elderly couple had their honeymoon picture on the front of their history book). In some of the booklets, photos were included with the text.

Home Office Computing: A Family Affair

Ross can't take full credit for all the money made in his computing endeavors: he is assisted by his wife Parmalee, who does much of the proofreading, polishing, line-editing and typing. Ross handles layout and content editing, computer mechanics such as sorting, conversions, doing labels, mail merges, etc.

- Place ads in writer's magazines and professional journals
- Post your brochure or flyer advertising services on university and graduate school bulletin boards
- Word-of-mouth from satisfied clients who were impressed with your services
- Mail cover letter, brochure, and business card to businesses
- Join professional and community organizations to meet people who will need your services
- Join Writer's Organizations in your city and state. Not only will you learn from programs and seminars, you will hear about opportunities for writers (e.g., publishers sometimes send projects to writer's organizations when they are looking for experienced writers)

Attend writer's conferences where you will meet publishers face-to-face, have your manuscripts critiqued, and network with all kinds of people in the writing and publishing business who may need your services.

Deciding Your Rates

How do you figure what to charge—by the whole project? Per page or an hourly rate? Ross advises comparing with other word-processing services, and asking those who work at advertising agencies and editors at publishing companies what they charge for certain projects. It's hard to know what to charge for a whole project fee, but many writers suggest that you decide on your hourly rate, then guess how long a job will take and double it. Check in writer's magazines for current per page rates. In addition, a good guide for pricing your writing is published in Writer's Market (available in bookstores and libraries, under the Reference Section).

> **Don't worry because the tide is going out—
> it always comes back.**
> —*Anonymous*

Purchasing Equipment Without Spending A Fortune

Avoid going into debt to purchase your computer, printer, and other office equipment for word processing. "If your business is dormant, or hits a low level of activity, you can ride it out and stay in business by going to work for temp agencies," Ross says. But if you take out a loan for a computer and color printer and you don't have work or you have a slow period, your equipment can get repossessed, and you've lost money *and* work.

If you already have an electronic typewriter or dedicated word processor, you have the equipment to start your business. As you get busier and have more work *and* the cash to buy a computer, there are definite advantages. Here are some ways to get the equipment you need at a lower-than-retail cost:

- Contact "User Groups" in your area by asking at computer stores and dealers that sell IBM, MacIntosh or the brand you're looking for. Also, check the Yellow Pages for "User Groups." By going to their once-a-month meetings, you can get used computer equipment, participate in "swaps," and find technical support when you run into problems with your computer. Many User Groups offer beginner's classes.

- Check the Classified Ads in your newspaper for used computers. "For word processing, even an IBM XT or other early IBM PC word processor will do, and you can do plenty of word processing without the font exchanges and bells and whistles the upgraded, newer models have—these are usually available for $200 or less," says Ross.

- Search computer magazines and discount computer stores and price everything so you know exactly what equipment and software costs. Then you can go to the local retailer and say, "I can get the Microsoft Word software for _____; if you can match that price, I'll buy it from you because I'd rather buy locally." Ross says he has never had a refusal from a legitimate offer like this; the local retailer has always matched it.

- If you know someone who is computer-wise, have them

help you shop at outlets. If you are patient and willing to look around, you can get a good package. My brother George, who's a great bargain shopper and very knowledgeable about electronics and computers, found my Tandy 4825 SX monitor, keyboard, and hard drive at a Tandy Outlet in Ft. Worth, Texas near his home for less than $1000 new, installed with the basic software I needed. My brother also helped me find the best prices on a fax, bubble-jet printer, and modem.

- If you have a friend who works at a bank or other larger business that "dumps" 12 or more computers at a time when they upgrade their whole system, tell him to call you when that happens! You can get a terrific computer package for a much lower-than-retail price.

Note: If your computer breaks down in the middle of a project, instead of racing out and making a hasty buy, go to a Quick-Print shop like Kinko where you can rent computer time for approximately $8 an hour. Take your disk and finish your project. (They are even open all night if you are really in a time crunch.)

Enhancing Your Skills

If you decide to begin a word processing business and your typing skills are rusty or you need to learn new word processing program, there are ways to enhance your skills and thus your productivity:

- Take advantage of the community colleges and Vo-Tech centers in your city or area by taking a course in Word Perfect, graphics and layout, How to Access the Internet, etc. Many of these computer courses are offered on Saturday (all day) or evenings and you can learn all the basic, intermediate, and advanced skills you need.

- Watch the newspaper for Business Conventions and Business Expos coming to your area. Office Supply stores often give free tickets to these events. Even if you don't have a ticket, large computer and software companies like

IBM, Lotus, and Microsoft offer free seminars and training workshops that are open to the public.

- Most word processing programs have excellent Tutorials so you can teach yourself. The Tutorial will introduce you to all the features of the program in a step-by-step fashion. Even if you attend a class, it's best to go through the Tutorial first.

Don't pin yourself into a stereotype of what you're going to do in your writing service. Beginning word processing business people must be willing to write almost anything. Later perhaps you could specialize if you find a profitable niche. One man started out with a brochure under his arm and samples of what he had done, then went to a business park. By knocking on doors, he met the director of a chain of hotels on the West Coast who just happened to need his services. First he did "elevator graphics," then moved on to menus for their hotel restaurants. He now does the menus for most of the restaurants in the Portland area. And it all started by knocking on doors in the business park.

Perhaps you are more suited to finding word processing work by networking with people or businesses you already know. Let them know what you do; give them a business card or your brochure. As Ross says, "It's who you know; and after that, it's what you know." All of his jobs he has gotten, aside from the *Writer's Digest* ads, have been through his network of people. "Once people know what you do, they will approach you for your skills."

In all your dealings with people, don't see them as just potential income. "I'm all for profit, but keep relationships above profit," Ross adds.

Avoid "Get Rich Quick" Schemes

When your home business is struggling and bills are mounting up, it is at this time that you will be most susceptible to the "Get Rich Quick" schemes. They will come across your path—offers and opportunities that are too good to be true. Mega money with mini effort. The focus will be on the money to be made. The fog will be on actual effort required. You will be told that it is "perfectly legal." "I have taken several of the 'perfectly legal' mail order programs and job opportunities to the Postmaster in Portland. The Postmaster didn't okay any of them," says Ross.

Avoid "Get Rich Quick" schemes and offers. Check them out with the Postmaster, the Better Business Bureau, and your common sense. Avoid them, and get on with working diligently to build a successful home-based business.

Recommended Resources

Writer's Digest magazine, with articles that challenge you to write, and articles that inspire and motivate you to keep going, to improve your craft of writing, and classified ads that will give you ideas.

The Art of Desktop Publishing—Using the Personal Computer to Publish it Yourself by Tony Bove (Bantam) and *Word Processing Profits at Home* by Peggy Glenn (Aames-Allen) Check your library for this and other resources on desk-top publishing and computer businesses.

To learn the secrets of the best computer whizzes and information you need to know about computers, I consulted with Tom Lough, a LEGO-Dacta executive and computer expert, and discovered seven important SUG-GESTIONS:

Top Computer Information For Home-Based Businesses

1. *Stay up to date with computer developments.* Visit your local library and read the computer magazines each month. Check on the computer courses available through your community college, especially if they are offered by a business and industry insti tute. By staying current, you will have a better understanding of what computers can do for your business.

2. *Buy a modem and subscribe to an online service,* such as CompuServe or America Online. Telecommunications has alredy begun to change the way the world does business. You can participate in professional discussion groups online. You can establish and nurture an electronic network. You can tap into an incredible amount of research and information online. You can have your manuscripts critiqued, market products, build business relationships, and find customers for your services. (See Appendix for 800 numbers of online services that you can get 10 or more free hours of online time to try out the service and see if it will enhance your business, and resources which can introduce you to the Internet.)

3. *Do not purchase software upgrades automatically.* Always check on the system requirements. Your current computer might not be able to run the latest upgrade. For example, your computer might not have sufficient random access memory (RAM) to run the more recent software. If your current software fills your needs, then perhaps purchasing an upgrade is not necessary. However, if the upgrade includes several new features that will increase your productivity, then you might want to give it serious consideration.

4. *How much memory is enough?* It is possible to add more random access memory (RAM) to most modern personal computers. This usually has the advantages of being able to run more complex programs, being able to handle large files easier (as in word processor documents of many pages), and sometimes being able to run several programs at once. Many of these advantage increases your productivity, so it might pay to investigate the purchase and installation of additional RAM. For many new computers, 4 to 8 megabytes of RAM is the standard minimum.

5. *Make "back-ups" a way of life.* Sooner or later, every hard disk drive must fail. When this happens, will you have

copies of all of your important files on other disks? If your files are only on your hard disk as you are reading this, STOP! Make backup copies of all of your files right now. Floppy disks will do, but you might also want to investigate an economical backup system with a removable hard disk cartridge. Regardless, back-ups will protect your information if the hard disk blows up from computer failure, electrical interruptions, fire, or other events. The extra time and small cost of extra disks will be well worth it if you ever need to recover your files.

6. *Accept no substitutes.* Run only software that you have purchased or properly registered for. Pay attention to the terms of the software license agreement. Software publishers will continue to provide us with the best business software in the world but only if they can stay in business themselves. Please don't condone software piracy; play by the rules.

7. *Always be willing to give help.* Everyone has to start from the same point when learning how to use computers effectively. Doubtless, someone helped you along at some point. Return the favor. Take time to answer questions or to pass along a tip or shortcut you have found valuable.

9

From Idea to Market

Mom's Family Preserves

When Ruthann Winans of Carlsbad, California, sat with her children having "tea parties" complete with teapot, apple juice and her conversation basket full of questions, little did she know she was planting the early seeds for Mom's Family Preserves, a home and family business that would grow like wildfire, sell to gift stores nationwide, and even become international within the first year.

"The idea sprang out of my desire that my children would know that their thoughts and feelings were important to me, that we'd get to know each other better," Ruthann says. She wanted to make sure their growing-up years didn't fly by in a blur. Questions like:

- What makes someone a good friend?
- What is your favorite thing for us to do together as a family?
- What do you think God is like?

Sparked wonderful conversations. And week after week the late evening tea parties with one of her three children (the other two went to bed and looked forward to their turn at teatime) made great memories. Soon Ruthann was eager to share her idea with other mothers she knew.

The most important work you will do . . . will be within the walls of your own home.
—Harold B. Lee

One evening Ruthann attended a seminar on organizational and homemaking skills. Afterward, she shared her idea about her question basket and tea parties with the seminar speaker, who suggested she put the questions in a decorated jar and sell them.

A brainstorm of ideas followed. Ruthann thought about how she could package a question-filled jar in such a decorative way that women would want to keep it out on their dining tables and use it often to help their families communicate better.

From that evening, October 8, 1991, more thoughts and practical ideas came that catapulted this entrepreneur into action. From the beginning she took a team approach, using the best of her talents to develop the product and marketing strategies, and enlisting her artistic sister-in-law, Mara, to custom-design the watercolor artwork on the canning label. Linda, another sister-in-law and a computer whiz, helped edit and polish the 150 questions and then typeset all the questions. And sister-in-law Sue handled the business details

Here are a few questions to ask yourself when you have a great idea for a new product or service you hope to market:

Developing Your Creative Ideas

- Is there a need for my product or service?
- Who is my market, or who will buy my product?
- How will I market my product?

Developing The Prototype

Ruthann spent an entire year developing the product. First she searched craft stores and purchased a plastic jar, designed a label, and gave the design to Mara to polish and professionalize. The fabric store was Ruthann's next stop, where she picked out country gingham fabric and ribbon. She glued a fabric square on the lid and added coordinating ribbon around the rim.

With four different jars in mind: "Mom's Canned Questions," "Mom's Delicious Devotional Questions," "Mom's Candied Christmas Fun," and "Mom's Pickled Predicament," she got four coordinating fabrics and matching colors of card stock for the questions.

Then came the hardest part: creating and polishing the 150 question or activity cards for each jar and doing all the research and comparison shopping to get the very best prices on materials and service. It took Ruthann months to find a printer that would print her questions for the price she could afford. Finding another printer to do the color separation on the label took extra time. After researching fabric prices, she found a company where she could buy fabric wholesale. And six months more went into developing the second jar.

Money-Saving Tips On Purchasing Services And Materials

Do Your Homework!

Research and look around to get the *lowest price* for quality raw materials and service such as printing or typesetting. Though it may take more time to shop around, it's worth it because every penny counts! So watch your costs without compromis ing quality.

Buy In Bulk—Save Money

When you buy in bulk, the cost per item is lower. If you order 100 flyers, you may find that ordering 500 you're only paying $20 more for the extra 400 flyers.

In the meantime, after several tries and experimenting with different formats, Ruthann put together a full-color marketing portfolio to present her products to store buyers. She then ordered raw materials in bulk: 383 large plastic jars, 40 yards of fabric, a few hundred yards of ribbon, 2000 sets of question cards and 2000 labels—all delivered to her garage.

Developing Your Product Brochure

- Visit trade shows and gift shows that sell products similar to yours
- Collect brochures and order forms as you look at booths
- After you get home, see which products you can remember from the brochure
- If you were a store owner, which brochures would stimulate

you to pick up the phone a week later and place an order for the products?

- Don't skimp on quality or color. Seasoned marketers say it's not worth doing a brochure unless it has a picture of your product, even if in black and white (color is even better if you can afford it). Remember a great brochure and product presentation translates into greater sales.

Putting together the first few hundred jars was truly a family affair. With the kitchen table as the center of production, the Winan children helped cut ribbon and painted glue on the jar lids. Ruthann and the sisters-in-law glued on fabric, ribbons, and bows. Husband Gary cut fabric and even their six-year-old got in the act as packer, putting all the finished jars in the boxes.

Marketing Mom's Family Preserves

The first orders for Mom's Family Preserves jars were sent to the seminar leader who sold over 1000 jars on their book and resource table in the first few months. At the same time Ruthann began showing the jars to buyers in local gift stores. She also sent samples of the jars to stores and individuals who might be interested in ordering the new product, which led to the mail order catalog "Best to You" carrying the jars. The company grew so rapidly that a new problem was created—the need for extra hands to assemble jars.

At this point, Ruthann contracted with 10 mothers who wanted to remain at home with their young children yet welcomed a chance for extra income. The homeworkers were paid a specific amount per assembled jar. This enables them to work at their own pace, be present to raise their children, and contribute to their household income. They pick up the product materials, go home to assemble, and return the finished product ready for shipment. That number has grown to 12 regular homeworkers and swells to a larger number during pre-holiday rush.

Rapid growth brought re-evaluation and a review of the obstacles yet to face. For although Mom's Family Preserves was experiencing early success, because the product had a low profit margin per jar, they needed to sell *high volume* in order to make the enterprise pay for the time and investment expended.

The Next Step: Exhibiting At Trade Shows

The Mom's Family Preserves staff made the decision to present their line nationwide at two large trade shows: Christian Bookseller's Association Convention in Atlanta and Beckman Gift Show in Los Angeles. This step involved additional investment to set up a booth, decorate it attractively, and present the products in the most professional fashion.

Creating Winning Trade Show Booths And Displays

- Pick a theme which matches your product
- Visit trade shows and study trade magazines and retail stores (like
- "Bath & Body Works"—a great user of props and little scenes to display products). See how the pros use color, props, and other features to enhance their products

- When you shop, look at other product displays to stimulate ideas
- What makes people stop at a booth? Color and motion are at the top! (Examples: In handmade basket booth—owner weaving basket; TV set in a booth with video presentation of product. One Mom's Family Preserves booth was designed as a garden scene. Water poured from a watering can accompanied by a sign that read, "Serve your family the living water.")
- Even if you just display your products on a table, buy a cloth and skirting at a party supply store for a professional look. Laminate letters of reference and newspaper articles about your business to add credibility.

- Make sure all signs have big, visible lettering; vinyl letters in all colors are available at office supply and art stores
- Make sure you plan a center or focus in your booth that eye level
- Before packing your materials to ship or drive to the trade show, set up the display in your garage. "There are so many details in a booth," says Ruthann. "We set it up, look at it, rearrange things, and get it just right before shipping it to the trade show. There you must be ready to set up quickly and efficiently, with all props, products, everything at your fingertips."

Trade Show Savvy

The vital part comes when you arrive at the trade show and set up your exhibit booth: making the most of the prospects that walk by your booth. Several tips which will improve your sales and follow-up orders are:

1. *Bring a stool.* This sounds like a silly thing to bring, but after several hours of standing in your booth talking with potential customers, fatigue often sets in and you may look for the nearest chair. Instead, bring a *stool* which you can sit or lean on and still be at eye level to answer questions or welcome people to your booth. (People walking by don't like to disturb a resting exhibitor.)

2. *Bring some help.* Since it is exhausting to talk to every person who walks by your booth (a good goal, since studies show that only one in 20 visitors is a hot prospect and you don't want to miss that *one*), bring a co-worker or several if possible to give you an opportunity for short breaks to renew your energy.

3. *Avoid standing at the entry of your booth.* If you are blocking the entry, it tends to intimidate customers and they will keep walking rather than stop to see your products and possibly place an order.

4. *Be a welcoming presence.* Appear just as warm and glad to see the customers as if you were welcoming them into

your home. Avoid folding your arms across your chest in
a way that says, "Don't bother me." Also, don't get into
long chats with your co-workers in the booth because most
people hate to interrupt people involved in a conversation.

5. *Prepare your presentation.* You have a very short time to
sell your products to the prospective customer who visits
your booth, so prepare an under-five minute presentation
of the benefits of your products. Make sure those helping
in the booth know the benefits also so they can
communicate them to prospects if you are away from the
booth. Avoid a hard-sell, but encourage a follow-up
meeting and make sure the prospect gets your brochure,
catalog, and order form.

The response to Ruthann's very professionally done displays
and products at the trade shows was overwhelming, and orders were
taken from stores all over the U.S. and even Europe. When she first
began her home-based company, Ruthann had been a full-time
homemaker for 14 years, with no business experience. So, to have
done so well at the trade shows was a milestone for her.

Valuable Tips For Product Development and Marketing

With six products, her business now ships 1000 jars a month.
The Mom's Family Preserves line is in over 650 stores in the U.S.,
Canada, Germany, England, and Central America. "If I can do it
anyone can," says Ruthann. The following is a sampling of what
she learned along the road to success.

Moving From Creative Idea To Prototype To Market

- *Cultivate patience,* and always expect things to take longer
than you think to produce. Your integrity is on the line if
you promise a store a certain date for products to be
shipped and can't deliver by a certain deadline.

- *Get Feedback.* Ask family, friends, and people in your area
of service or product for honest feedback on your product.
If you get negative responses but still have a gut feeling
your idea is a promising one—proceed!

Also get feedback on your product displays and marketing materials. Set up props with the products and create a vignette, take photos, and show them to people you know to get input on how to improve.

- *Anticipate Obstacles.* Don't get too discouraged when you meet up with obstacles. If you believe in your product, don't let anything stop you. Every business has problems and challenges. "I've learned to expect obstacles and then to jump over them," says Ruthann. In the midst of difficulties, what keeps her going is her concern for the American family and her belief that Mom's Canned Questions could help "preserve" family life by strengthening communication between parents and children.

In due season, we shall reap if we do not lose heart.
—The Bible

- *Ask lots of questions of successful people.* Talk about your idea with as many people as possible. Then, evaluate their feedback. Read books on business in general and in your particular field. You will get a better perspective on what you are doing.

- *Get a partner.* Having a partner helps with the start-up costs as well as the work load. It works best if one person handles the business while the other handles the creative side. In Mom's Family Preserves, Ruthann does what she does best: idea-developing, design, display, and marketing strategies. Sue, her partner, is the business manager. Her responsibilities include day-to-day functions of processing and fulfilling orders.

- *Keep your sense of humor!* You'll need it as the business grows. Look for humorous comic strips to post on your office bulletin board; watch an old comedy movie video now and then in the evening; most of all, don't take yourself or your business too seriously. Once in a while, shut the door on your office and have some fun! You will return to your office or studio refreshed and ready to create.

- *Keep a notebook handy.* If you have bursts of creativity,
  make a place for the care and feeding of your best ideas!
  A small notepad in the car, by your bed, kitchen counter,
  and even bathroom is necessary for recording ideas and
  "catching" those brainstorms about products or strategies
  which are going to make your business grow. "I'm so
  thankful that God has given me a creative mind!" says
  Ruthann. "I always keep a notepad next to me to jot down
  ideas as they come."

When you are in the planning and designing stage of your
trade show booth or product display for stores, have a spiral
notebook with you to jot down ideas on design, layout, concept or
format. The way props are used and products are displayed can
inspire you to learn how to enhance your own products.

"You can have the best product in the world," says Ruthann,
"but if it is not packaged and displayed to its best advantage, it
won't sell." She likes the idea of setting up little vingettes with
props like a table covered with a patchwork quilt, a white wicker
chair, and a natural woven basket filled with the jars. Her vignette
creates a homey, family atmosphere that welcomes buyers into her
booth. The vignette and props also give the store owners great ideas
on how to best display her products in their stores.

"Since my product is a kitchen item, we surround it with
farm-fresh, kitchen decor," says Ruthann. "I carefully studied trade
magazines to see how others used props to enhance their products
and create a booth so inviting that people would stop to look. I
wanted people to remember our products from the full-color brochure, and order even a week or two after the show." The strategy
worked!

Like most home business people, you may not have a marketing team to brainstorm about how to best display your product. But
with some creativity, feedback from family and friends, a passion
for the product, (*and* the ideas in this chapter), you can create
winning displays.

Learn From Your Mistakes

All new businesses have an element of "learning experience" and trial and error mixed in. Mistakes are normal. But as Mom's Family Preserves did, *learn from your mistakes*. Here's one mistake you can *prevent* if you profit from Ruthann's experience.

"The hardest lesson I've learned is *don't ever assume anything on services or products ordered and make sure everything is written down in detail and signed by both parties,*" she says. This one principle could save you hundreds of dollars!

When a new set of questions were ready to be typeset, the printer printed a few pages and ran the pages through the cutter. Then he realized part of the copy was cut because the alignment was slightly off. However, to save time and meet the deadline, he suggested a typesetter realign the already typeset questions.

Ruthann gave the go-ahead to use the recommended typesetter's services and they agreed on a price over the phone to realign the questions. The printer then gave the typesetter directions. But unfortunately, the new typesetter, without Ruthann's knowledge, retyped all of the questions and set them in correct alignment. In the process, she made many typographical errors, and did not have the copy proofread before it was handed back to the printer—a mistake that cost the business $2,400.

"I should have met with the typesetter and given specific instructions, in writing, on exactly what was expected, no matter what the deadline was," says Ruthann. It is also important to insist on proofreading the final copy *before* the print run is started. Don't ever assume people know what you are talking about when you give instructions. And don't be in too big a hurry when printing is involved. Give yourself time to get a perfect, polished copy.

The Adventure Of A Lifetime

Even with the hectic pace of running a fast-growing company and handling the inevitable problems, developing and marketing the Mom's Family Preserves line of products is a great adventure for Ruthann. Although she gives credit to God for the gift of creative ideas and her husband and family for their support and help, the business wouldn't be alive without her enthusiasm and willingness to risk and to try something totally new.

"When I had the idea for Mom's Family Preserves I knew if I didn't at least try to get it off the ground, I'd look back someday as I rocked in my rocking chair wondering what would have happened *if only I had taken the chance* . . .now I know!" For more information (800) 771-MOMS, P. O. Box 725, Carlsbad, CA 92018

Trade Journals For The Giftware Business

Excellent resources for researching and studying the marketplace, planning exhibits and displays

Gifts and Decorative Accessories
51 Madison Avenue
New York, NY 10010-1675

Giftware News
Talcott Communications
20 North Walker Drive
Suite 3230
Chicago, IL 60606-9687

Country Business
P. O. Box 408
St. Charles, IL 60174

Christian Retailing
Subscription Service Department
P. O. Box 465
Mt. Morris, IL 61054-7697

10

Building A Successful Consulting Business

Roberts & Associates, CPA

"Leanne Roberts, CPA, formerly of Hogan & Slovacek, and George Roberts, MS, Computer Science, have teamed to form Roberts & Associates, CPA, a certified public accounting firm dedicated to providing their clients the best in creative, pro-active, personalized tax and consulting services," said the news item in the *Tulsa World* business section.

Leanne and George just happen to be a husband-and-wife team whose areas of expertise include all types of income tax return preparation, especially for individuals, trusts, and oil and gas entities; retirement, estate, and personal financial planning; small business consulting; and computer system analysis, design, and implementa tion. What a team!

One December, Leanne left the large CPA firm where she had been employed for seven years and began her own home-based accounting/consulting firm with her husband. "If you are a tax accountant, the best time to leave is in December; otherwise, you won't get any business," says Leanne. She used the slow time from January to February to get organized and set up in her home office before the super-busy tax preparation time hit.

The reason Leanne left the CPA firm and went into business for herself had to do with her philosophy of serving clients and a desire to spend more time with her family. "A lot of clients couldn't afford the fees of a large accounting firm. I felt caught in the middle between what was best for the client or the company, and that created pressure." In addition, she and her supervisors had different management styles. As Leanne "grew up" to management, it was time to see if she could do it on her own.

Leanne, who had earned the highest score in the state of Oklahoma on the November, 1987, CPA exam, had built a large base of clients while working at the firm. Several clients came with her for the lower fees she was able to offer in the new practice. Since Leanne has lower overhead costs, does not charge for travel time, and offers the convenience of going to the client's place of business or home to consult on their taxes and accounting needs, her clients are getting more of her time and more personal service.

Husband George, who has a Masters of Science degree in Computer Science, has worked as a software writer, creating both software tools and consumer applications. In the new business George handles client computer problems.

The Consulting Field

Professional consulting is a wide-open field available to those who have specific expertise in a particular area. Some consulting positions, such as Certified Public Accountant, legal, medical, environmental and engineering consultation, require licensing. On the other hand, there are fields that do not require special licensing (educational, career, wedding, financial aid, or even small business).

Consulting businesses have relatively low overhead and high income potential. But even with the skills and special ability to be a consultant, your business will not grow unless you master the ability to market your service.

How To Market Your Consulting Service

"First, you have to have a plan for getting clients and keeping them," says Leanne. She advises telling everyone you know about you business, asking them for referrals, and handing out your business card every chance you get. "Your business card is the first step," she adds. Keep them with you and give to friends, relatives, and potential clients.

Network with others by joining the Chamber of Commerce professional and community organizations in order to meet potential clients. Join organizations where people need your service. Along with other community organizations, Leanne joined the local and state Home-Based Business Association where she became Treasurer; she also presented a program on taxes for home-based business men and women.

In both your business card, brochure, and other information you distribute about your consulting service, be very specific about what you offer and how it benefits your client. In Roberts & Associates' case, they sent a mailing on letterhead with the following information:

- Mission
- Expertise
- Background
- Fee Structure
- Expectations

Their mission statement clearly set out what their business philosophy and services provided, and emphasized that they are "dedicated to providing our clients the best in creative, pro-active, personalized tax and consulting services."

In the "Fee Structure" section, they highlighted one of the benefits to clients—a flexible billing method:

"It is customary for public accounting firms to charge by the hour for their services. For many projects it is difficult to estimate accurately the time that will be required to complete them. By billing by the hour, you pay for only the actual time, and we are compensated for all the time spent on your project.

"Many Clients prefer the certainty of a fixed fee arrangement. You agree to a price and know that, barring unforeseen complications, this is the price you will pay regardless of whether it takes us more or less time than estimated to complete your project. Roberts & Associates, CPA will use whichever method you prefer . . ."

In the *Expectations* they further explain the benefits to their clients: "We believe that Roberts & Associates can offer better service at more affordable rates. We would like to work *with* you (not just *for* you) to generate ideas that will improve your situation. In return, if you are satisfied with our services, please tell your friends and associates about us . . ."

This kind of mailing produced several new clients and referrals. The more specific you can be about the value of your service, the better.

You can also gain an identity professionally and add new clients by offering to do seminars and public speaking for the types of people and organizations that would use your service, by sending out a newsletter quarterly, bi-monthly, or monthly with, in the case of an accounting consulting business such as Roberts & Associates: tax tips, tax deductions for home offices, six tips on writing a business plan, etc.

"When we fail to plan we set ourselves up for failure."

Getting Started In A Consulting Business

Here's the best advice Leanne *didn't* take, at least not at first: **Have A Business Plan.** "It's too easy when you're working at home to not get anything accomplished, to garden or grocery shop,

Have a Business Plan— Set Goals

so **Set Goals**—that's what a business plan is. A business plan should define your income goals and identify clients you are seeking. Thus, your goals are more concrete. "And seeing if what I'm doing today or this week is leading me towards my goals expressed in the business plan, or if I'm

being sidetracked by the urgent. If you've got a plan, you are more likely to meet your goals," says Roberts. Plan on paper, and plan in detail.

Areas Your Business Plan Should Cover

- A mission statement or list of objectives
- Income plan (revenue you hope to generate in a year)
- Working goals (To work eight hours a day, five days a

week imposes structure, from which most people benefit. Your working goals might include being in the office by 8 a.m. every morning and making a list of what to accomplish each day.) "I make sure there is something revenue-generating on that list *every day,*" says Roberts.

- Plan for funding your business, whether that includes borrowing, getting financial backers, or other methods. "It's a good idea not to get over your head in debt," Leanne says. "I have a client that is thousands of dollars in debt. He went out on a limb, bit off more than he could chew in buying a hair salon, and now is not making any money." Being undercapitalized is a common pitfall for home and small businesses. If you need advice in this area, consult with a CPA or experienced business person.

- Market research: *Who* are your customers? *Where* are they? *Who* are your competitors? *How* is your business distinctive from theirs?

- Start-up costs: materials, equipment, licenses and fees, insurance, taxes, business cards and advertising, phone or answering service,professional stationery, office supplies, computer, modem, etc.

- A plan for getting clients and promoting your service (where and how you will advertise)

- A five-year plan (Think about what you hope to accomplish not just this year, but several years down the road.)

- Your fee schedule

Your business plan is usually requested when you apply for a bank or small business loan. But whether you finance the business yourself or are funded in part by a backer or silent partner, invest the time it takes to write a comprehensive business plan—your blue-print for success—and you'll be one step closer to achieving it.

Resources For Business Plans

An inexpensive publication on how to develop a business plan: *The Business Plan for Homebased Business,* available from

The Small Business Administration, P. O. Box 15434, Ft. Worth, TX 76119

Roberts & Associates recommends *The Arthur Young Business Plan Guide,* Seigel, Schultz, Ford and Carney (John Wiley & Sons, 1987)

HOME-BASED BUSINESS: Putting It All Together contains an easy-to-prepare but thorough business plan, plus pricing information, marketing research, and much more. (published by Office for Entrepreneurship, Oklahoma State University, Stillwater, OK 74078-0337)

More Good Advice For Consulting Businesses

Leanne advises that you choose a business in which you not only have experience and knowledge, but one that you enjoy. Because, if you don't like what you're doing, you won't do it. "I'd never have a job where I dreaded going to work," she says. "Life is too short for that.

"Start slowly and plan well. Don't bite off more than you can chew." Decide how many hours you want to work and do no more. If you're consulting at home, the temptation is to take all the work. But if you have small children, you can't work 60 hours a week and still have time for your children. "The temptation is to say yes to everything and take on too much work."

Most importantly *don't bid too low for your consulting services.* The client always wants to know your fee schedule up front. And you need to decide, "Can I afford to do this?" When confronted with a client who is in a tight situation and needs your help, you may say, "I'll do it for nothing, or at this low price because you can't afford my fee.

"But unfortunately," confides Leanne, "if people don't pay, they don't usually appreciate the service. And if you aren't paid, you won't be in business for long." Here is a way to figure your fee for service.

Start by considering the value of your time, expertise, and knowledge/experience. Add in your direct costs, overhead costs, and profit for investment and future business expansion. "No one would ask you to sell a product at less than your cost, even if asking you to donate it, they pay your cost," Roberts says.

For those in service businesses, customers often ask you to give away your service for nothing, not realizing that not only are you giving away your time, but also your overhead (your computer, paper, phone expenses, all the out-of-pocket expenses it takes to be in business).

You have to get a clear understanding of your overhead costs that need to be included in the service fee, and here's how Leanne advises you do it: consider electricity, office equipment, taxes, insurance, and all the above. Figure out for a month or year what expenses you paid (or will pay). Add up your invoices and receipts for all expenses, both bills and out-of-pocket. Then figure approximately how many hours a year you will be billing time. If you give speeches, figure the 100 hours per year you are going to speak, or the 1,500 hours you are going to bill for tax consulting. Then by dividing the number of hours into the total cost you will learn the per-hour cost of your time.

Therefore, if asked to speak or consult by a church or non-profit organization, you can say: "I can do this for you, but I have certain fixed costs I have to recover, so I will need to be compensated $5 an hour." Or if you are figuring speaking fees, add in preparation time for speaking (four hours for each one hour of speaking). So in figuring 400 hours for 100 hours of speaking, you could say, "I'll give you a one-hour speech, at $6 an hour for expenses."

Tax Tips For Home-Based Businesses

Tax laws are constantly changing and sometimes are confusing, so it's in your best interest to get professional help in preparing them for the IRS. But there are some important basic tax tips for you to follow in your home business. Adhere to these tax tips offered by Roberts & Associates and it will make it easier to file your tax return, know where you stand financially, and make decisions.

HOME BUSINESS HAPPINESS
Building a Successful Consulting Business

1. *Choose the way you organize your business.* (Partnership, S-Corporation, etc.) You should consider more than just the tax consequences of entity type. (See Appendix for Different Types of Business Structures, their advantages and disadvantages.)

2. *Run your business like a business, not like a hobby.* That doesn't mean you can't have fun. It means you must try to make a profit.

3. *Set up your home business space carefully, so that it meets the IRS rules for home office deduction.* Generally, your space must be used exclusively (i.e., only for business) and regularly (ie., not just occasionally). You have to be able to show that your home office is the *principal place of business.* That is determined by the importance of the business activity done at home versus other locations; and the percent of time spent at home.

   The procedure to figure your home office deduction is: take the square footage of the house and divide it into the square footage of your office space and get the percentage Then deduct that percentage from your household expenses (rent, utilities, etc.) as a business expense.

   Even if you don't plan to take the deduction, you will work more efficiently if you have a separate space and you never know when you may need the deduction.

4. *Choose whether to use the cash or accrual method of accounting.* If you have inventory, you must use the accrual method, at least for the inventory. That means that you cannot deduct the cost of the inventory until you sell it.

5. *Keep accurate, consistent, timely records.* Do not wait until you have time to do recordkeeping. Do it now. Reconcile your bank statement every month.

6. *Calculate and pay quarterly estimated tax payments.* It is likely that you taxes will be 50% of your net income (not gross receipts). Budget for this and pay it when due.

7. *Don't pay workers as independent contractors unless they really are.* Unless you know they are a corporation, get their social security number before you pay anyone for services. This includes your yard service, maid service, and attorney; anyone who is a business expense for you. You are required to file Form 1099—Misc. if you paid someone $600 or more for services for your business.

8. *If you have employees, let a service (such as Paychex or ADP) handle your payroll.* The service will prepare all the forms that need to be filed and tell you who to pay when. They can do it much more accurately and efficiently than you can. Paying your payroll taxes on time should be a "Number One priority."

9. *If you are selling a product, you probably need a sales tax permit.* This permit allows you to buy your inventory and manufacturing equipment without paying sales tax on it. (However, it does not allow you to buy office supplies or equipment without paying sales tax.) If you buy office supplies or equipment through the mail, you are probably required to pay use tax. Even if you do not have a sales tax permit, you obligated to collect and remit sales tax on the items you sell.

"Those steps are the basics," says Leanne. Once you have the basics covered the following should be considered:

- Start a retirement savings plan. There are several kinds from which to choose (eg., IRA, SEP, 401[K]), one of them should work for your situation. The amounts you save are generally deductible to your business.

- Employ your children under 18 years old. You don't have to pay FICA on their wages.

- Generally, you can expense (i.e., write—off or deduct) up to $17,500 each year in furniture and equipment that you otherwise would have to capitalize and depreciate. This does not include buildings, and because of limitations on deductions for autos, it is usually not helpful to use it for autos.

- Keep a log in each car. Write down the date, where you are going, why (if it is not obvious from the "where") and how many miles, round trip. Trips to the store to buy office supplies count.

There are usually no simple answers to tax or other business questions. Find a good adviser and keep in touch with her or him at least once a month. When in doubt about questions such as if your home office qualifies for tax breaks or if you have held out enough for quarterly taxes, consult a professional tax consultant.

Improving Quality Of Life

For Leanne, one benefit of being in private practice and home-based is she can maintain a much better *balance* in her life. She has enough clients that she can work six to eight hours a day and get it all done, yet make enough money to live.

Leanne walks two miles a day listening to a cassette tape or with family members. "My daughter gets home from school between 1:30 and 2:00 in the afternoon, and I stop working so that we can visit for half an hour or an hour." Since Leanne's husband works at home, she sees him more. Her evenings are free, unless there's an evening meeting to attend or a project due the next day.

Leanne has much more time than when she was working 12 to 18 hours a day for the firm, and she even has more hours with her family during the busy tax season. Thus, her health and disposition have improved. "I don't get depressed anymore or have to take vitamin B6 to keep from getting run down and depressed. I used to have a rash over my body from a very stressful job," she adds. She has more control of her time than when she was with the firm.

"Stress is worse, primarily when you feel you don't have control of your work situations," she says. Her present consulting business has deadlines and stress like any business, but not stress which is not damaging to her health or family life. Leanne and George are getting along better because "he appreciates what I do and we spend more time together—which helps our relationship develop." Her daughter is happier because she gets to see Leanne, even during the busy season. Before, Leanne would have to leave for the office before 6:00 a.m. and would not get home until 10 p.m. when her daughter was in bed. "They didn't see me much from February to April," and even in the non-tax time, not until 8:00 at night.

When husband and wife work together, as the Roberts do, it's important to maximize your strengths instead of sticking to old, traditional roles. Her best advice to a married couple working together in a home business: *Find out what each one's strengths are and use them.* Don't try to

Working With Your Spouse

make the other person into something they aren't. George, for example, is never going to be an accountant. Besides being a computer expert, he is Leanne's secretarial support: he does all the word processing, all transmittal letters, and filing instructions for tax returns and billings.

George is also is strong in analyzing situations and coming up with creative ideas to solve problems. So Leanne discusses a clients' tax problems with him, and he brainstorms with her, usually coming up with ideas to solve it. Then she, with the accounting background, decides what will work or not. "He gives me a lot of ideas I'd never think of. It's always good to brainstorm about problems because you come up with more ideas, some of them ridiculous." Sometimes the ridiculous ideas are the best, most creative solutions that *do work,* even though at first they sound crazy.

Creative problem-solving: that's what the Roberts hope the hallmark of their business will be, providing creative financial and tax planning ideas for clients and businesses. A lot of people can prepare tax returns; but what clients need is someone to think about their situation and how to improve it.

Filling a niche that no one else can and identifying the need—that's what makes any business successful.

Resources For Consulting Businesses

*The Complete Guide to Consulting Success,*Howard Shenson and Ted Nicholas;Iincludes agreements and forms, (Chicago: Dearborn Financial Publishing, Inc. 1993)

Consultant's News (Monthly newsletter) 603-585-6544

Consulting Opportunities Journal, Bimonthly journal: how to get started, set fees, market your service, Gapland, MD 21736

Consultants and Consulting Organizations Directory. Gale Research Company (Check your public library in the reference section)

Periodicals For The Home-Based Accountant

Because it is harder to talk to your peers about technical topics when you are isolated in a home-based accounting office, it is even more important to keep up with the journals that cover your specialties. Following is a list of Roberts & Associates favorite periodicals:

The Tax Adviser

Estate Planning

Trusts & Estates

Accounting Today

Journal of Accountancy

Book: *On Your Own! How To Start Your Own CPA Firm,* Albert S. Williams. (Published by AICPA, the American Institute of Certified Public Accountants.

11

Adapting Priceless Treasures & Old Lace to Modern Wear

The Maryon Allen Company

"It all started when I was a child," says Maryon Allen, expert textile restoration artist, widow of the former U.S. Senator James B. Allen, and president of the unique company that bears her name. "My grandmother started me sewing when I was two years old while she was making flapper garters for my mother. She let me string the beautiful gold Venetian glass beads on the garters, and I haven't put a needle down since." Maryon has done sewing and needlework of almost every kind her whole life.

In fact, needlework was a "lifesaver" to her at one point in her life. During 1967, she spent six months in a sanitarium after a bout with tuberculosis. Since the medication she took affected her concentration for reading, she turned to needlework. Crewel embroidery and needlepoint kept her busy for many hours during her recovery. She also taught a needlework class for other patients. "Sewing literally saved my sanity," says Maryon.

Laces And Treasures

It was her love for beautiful fabrics and treasured family heirloom clothes that sparked a very successful business known throughout the South and especially Alabama. "When we were living in Washington, D.C., I started buying old flapper and '20s ensembles, Edwardian turn-of-the-century and other vintage clothes from antique shops," Maryon says. *Antique* technically means 100 years old or older. She had also inherited some beautiful heirloom clothing which she restored and adapted to modern wear.

A Sense of Humor is Like a Needle and Thread; it Will Patch up Many Things.

"Our bodies have changed since the days these antique clothes were made. Women are larger in the rib cage and waists, instead of being confined in corsets like women used to be. Bust lines have changed and lingerie and underwear styles have changed through the years," she says.

Maryon, an expert self-taught artist with needle and thread, began adapting and altering the clothes, redesigning, cleaning, and wearing them to the many social events she and her Senator husband attended. She continued buying and collecting the clothing, as well as antique laces, linens, Chinese shawls, antique beaded bags and accessories. She has French ball gowns, a black silk opera coat with a train, Paris dresses—and when she wore the splendid restored clothing, people loved it.

The Cliff House

When Maryon returned to Alabama after completing her late husband's Senate term, she bought the Cliff House, a registered, historic home in Birmingham. A former columnist for *The Washington Post* for three years, she planned to write but was more interested in getting into linens, shawls, antique clothing and accessories. After restoring the old historic house, doing most of the work herself, she decided she must make sense of the bigness and expense of maintaining the mansion. So she decided to have a little shop as a tax write-off.

Maryon decorated the walls of her shop with a treasure trove of wonderful things: Spanish shawls, gorgeous laces, antique wedding gowns, and other vintage clothes. Suddenly people asked to buy the clothing. Maryon said, "You can't have mine, but I'll get you some." So she began to look for buyers to bring in antique clothes she could restore and sell. As word spread, people brought in sacks of heirloom lace, wedding gowns, and garments from days past. With a growing trend in the U.S. and other countries toward wearing authentic, vintage clothing, the restoration business grew.

The shop became secondary to the restoration, and textile restoration became the first and only business, as the Maryon Company, Inc. evolved into a vintage restoration company that is known today throughout the Southeast and the world. Maryon works at the restoration fulltime with two assistants. They have antique clothing from all over the world, and are booked solid on weddings for a year or more ahead.

As Maryon says, "There's a Southern question/joke that goes, 'Have you bought your wedding dress yet?' to which the bride-to-be answers, 'Oh, no, I'm wearing my mother's gown.'" (Translation: We've always had money to buy fine dresses in our family, not like the nouveau riche who go and buy one at a bridal shop!) Everyone wants to look like mother or grandmother now; it's a fad to wear an antique wedding gown and vintage clothes.

Restoring Antique Clothing

Restoration of old clothing is a tedious and time-consuming process. "There was no pit stop or cleaners in the Edwardian days," says Maryon. "People didn't bathe as frequently as we do or clean the clothes, so clothes were generally ruined. A heavy satin dress wouldn't be cleaned after the balls and parties. Its trains dragged all over the place, so it would arrive here filthy," she says.

There aren't any rules for the restoration Maryon does, no book that told her how to do it. "We do everything original, and make up the process on whatever needs to be done." Being an engineer's daughter, she has a natural innovative quality, and her sewing talent aids in the restoration of lace and other features. In one Edwardian gown which dated back to the late 1800s, Maryon restored the lace and replaced the silk taffeta lining—which had rotted away—with new lining. In addition, she made the train longer than it originally had been in order to protect the antique lace.

How long does it take to restore a wedding gown? "I washed wedding dresses all day yesterday," she says—two glorious 1930's silk and satin dresses, covered with orange stains from being stored wrong. The amount of time it takes to restore a vintage wedding gown is dependent upon its condition, but one with an average amount of damage may require approximately twenty hours of work to complete. First the piece is cleaned. Then lace is repaired, using matching remnants from other pieces of clothing. Stains that cannot be removed by cleaning are covered with lace. Her trademark, fabric roses, adorn the pieces she restores. Sometimes the fabric roses and lace are mixed with yards of matching ribbon and embellish a train for a wedding dress.

Besides the antique clothing and lace people bring to her in big garbage bags, Maryon buys antique clothing, slips and lace to use and design something from the pieces. In addition to the restoration work for clients, she has restored a dress from the 1870's for a Pennsylvania museum, and restored a Washington-family christening gown, now displayed in the Daughters of the American Revolution Museum in Washington, D.C. She also does the whole wedding for family members, nieces and granddaughters. As her gift, she dresses the bride in antique—restored lingerie, wedding gown, and all the trimmings. And if they don't want a vintage wedding dress, she creates an original.

In addition to clothing, Maryon Allen Company restores and redesigns tablecloths. There are only a few people in the United States that restore antique lace curtains or fine Belgian, French, or Swiss textiles. She does not reweave, but restyles and renovates the pieces.

"We never know what is coming in the door, as we get UPS packages from everywhere. We do priceless wedding veils from Venetia. We are sent an antique wedding dress found in Brussels or Switzerland that a family member wants restored," she says.

She has also gotten into christening dresses that she custom designs and creates called "Maryon's Royal Lengths." These christening dresses are very long and beautiful, just like you'd find in a cathedral for a royal christening. She gets calls from expectant mothers as far away as British Columbia and Alaska commissioning her to make their babies christening dresses even before they are born.

Maryon also uses her experience as a journalist and her expertise as a seamstress and textile restoration specialist to write a popular column for *McCall's Needlework* Magazine, called "Meticulous Details" on the care of fine fabrics. "Mail has come in from every country in the world," she says. "I've answered mail until I thought I'd die." With word-of-mouth promotion from satisfied customers, her magazine columns and publicity Maryon Allen Company has received, she has more than enough demand for her unique kind of service, and does not need to do any further advertising.

Secrets Of Success

"One important thing I learned in all those years in politics," Maryon says, is: *You Have to Please People.* She learned how to treat customers from her father, who was a successful Caterpillar-tractor dealer. "Dad taught me that the customer is always right, and if you don't have good *service,* you don't have a good business."

- "If you have good service," she adds, "people will come back and refer lots of people to you." Her best advice on customer relations:
- Treat the customer with *Courtesy, Compassion, and Kindness.*
- Use good manners
- Make customers feel welcome in your shop and treat them with graciousness
- Treat them as the only person who is important at the time they are there. If it's a one-hour appointment, that's their time, she says.
- Give your undivided attention, listen, and see what they want.

Maryon meets with customers "By Appointment Only." Walk-in trade, she feels, is a waste of time.

On the other hand, use good common sense in dealing with customers. "Don't let them owe you," she advises. "Have them pay in cash. Don't go with the credit card system, or extend credit. If you have a lot of accounts receivable, then you get into debt and have no cash flow. You can't take accounts receivable to the Bank!" She ships everything COD, and finds the greatest thrill in business is making deposits.

Use Your Talent and Act Like a Pro

If you have a talent, Maryon advises that you "act like a pro" and you'll help people respect your talent. Try to establish what your work is worth. State what you want, or your fee schedule, and stick to it.

"You must act like a *pro* instead of an amateur in every aspect. If you do something wrong, make it right. Believe in yourself and act professionally, whether you're hemming dresses or sewing for customers."

Finding Your Niche In Sewing

There are a myriad of possibilities if you have talent with a needle and thread and access to a sewing machine. Here are a few to consider:

- Quilt-making
- Alterations and tailoring
- Creating custom clothing for weddings, proms, and special occasions
- Designing and making your own product. One mom made and marketed a "Nursery Drape" for nursing mothers; another made bows.
- Sewing drapes, curtains, and other window treatments and matching bedspreads for interior decorators or individuals
- Furniture upholstery
- Custom-designed patterns for women, children, or infants

- Teaching sewing lessons

Sewing Organizations Or Associations

American Home Sewing Association/AHSA
1375 Broadway
New York, NY 10018

American Sewing Guild/ASG
Post Office Box 50936
Indianapolis, IN 46250

National Needlework Association (NNA)
650 Danbury Road
Ridgefield, CT 06877

American Needlepoint Guild (ANG)
728 Summerly Drive
Nashville, TN 37209

Resources For Seamstresses

Threads Magazine
Taunton Press
63 S. Main St., P. O. Box 355
Newtown, CT 06470
(800) 283-7252

McCall's Needlework
825 7th Avenue
New York, NY 10019
(212) 887-8435

The Complete Encyclopedia of Stitchery, Mildred Graves Ryan
Holbrook, MA: Adams Publishers, 1994

The Vogue/Butterick Step-By-Step Guide to Sewing Techniques
NY: Simon & Schuster, 1989

*Sew to Success: How to Make Money in a Home-Based Sewing
Business,* Kathleen Spikes (Available from *Threads* magazine)

Keeping Your Business Legal

The first thing to do when starting a sewing business (or any kind of business, for that matter), Maryon advises, is "Go directly to your CPA!" Tell him what you plan to do and then ask: What do I need to do? Ask for a list of regulations, permits, anything you must comply with to be legal. Obtain forms that must be filled out.

Ask for information on employees, sales tax, and everything. Get a tax number so you can buy wholesale.

However, she doesn't advise turning over the bookkeeping to someone else. "I'd never turn my business or bookkeeping over to anyone. I want to know what's happening in my business, and learn everything I need to know to run it successfully," she says.

Maryon also advises a Personal Checking Account and a separate Company Account. Not only does it help your mind become more orderly, it will help you at tax time. Establish a good credit rating and good reputation with banks. And become a member of the Better Business Bureau. "The Better Business Bureau puts out a wonderful newsletter with all kinds of information you can use. Being a member shows you are approved and helps you maintain a good reputation."

The Better Business Bureau

> Council of Better Business Bureaus, Inc.,
> 1515 Wilson Boulevard,
> Arlington, VA 22209

Look in the Yellow Pages of your phone directory for the local Better Business Bureau. You can register your company if you fill out a questionnaire have a license for your business. Attach letters from satisfied customers, and include positive news articles about your business.

> Maryon Allen Company, Inc.
> The Cliff House
> 3215 Cliff Road
> Birmingham, AL 35205

12

Nurturing and Developing Great Ideas from Concept To Market

Goosecreek Enterprises: The Card-Well Tray

On a sunny Texas Saturday in 1989, after deciding that collecting baseball cards would make a good hobby for the whole family, Tammy and Jack Cardwell came home from Sam's, a wholesale and discount store, with six boxes of Topps baseball cards. They immediately began sorting the 3,240 cards, unaware that they were about to embark on a great business adventure. After sorting the cards for about an hour, and with hundreds of cards in neat little stacks on the floor, they cringed as their two-year-old son, Terry, accidentally knocked over several stacks.

"There has to be a better way to do this." Creative at heart, Jack began sketching ideas on paper and came up with a plan for a baseball-card sorting tray. He purchased balsa wood, which is light-weight and easy to cut and shape, and made a prototype. As he used the prototype baseball-card sorting tray, he discovered what was right and wrong about it. He also let some friends use it, and soon they were discussing the possibility of manufacturing the tray to market.

Jack had a desire to market the tray and believed it would sell, but he didn't know how to start. So first he did research on the feasibility of producing the tray, and figured all the costs involved. "I quickly realized that capital would be my main obstacle," said

Jack. He estimated the cost of tooling the mold at somewhere between $5,000 to $15,000, a large amount of money when you don't have it!

The Search For Capital

After thinking about the way to raise the capital needed for the venture, the two friends with whom he had shared an interest in card-collecting agreed to be partners and help supply the money to develop, manufacture, and advertise the product and keep the business going until a return was realized on their investment.

At the same time, Jack conferred with several plastics plants about the best way to produce a durable, high-quality tray at a low cost. The second prototype emerged from the suggestions of these people in the plastics industry and his friends who collected cards. This prototype tray was then used for a period of time to make sure it worked well.

Next, the three partners pooled their resources, and Jack found a plastics company in Dallas, who agreed to help him produce the tray on a tight budget. "The manager was very helpful with the technical aspects of the production," says Jack. After several discussions with him, Jack generated a set of drawings, and after several modifications at the plant, a final design emerged and the cost for tooling and production was projected.

The process of getting the $12,000 actually took several months. As soon as they had the money for the tooling of the tray, it was sent to Precision Formed Plastics Company. Then, as additional money came in, it was used for whatever was needed at that point.

Profiting From Mistakes

Even with the extensive research the Cardwells did and the eight months of developing the prototype, inevitable mistakes were still made. "But we learned a great deal from those mistakes!" Tammy adds. For instance, in their first shipment, they made mistakes in packaging. Too many trays were packed to a case, putting too much weight on the bottom trays. Breakage was the result.

The Cardwells then went to heavier boxes which held fewer trays and when packed upside down to even out the weight distribution, helped prevent breakage. The trays are now made of a thicker plastic that contains a rubberizer to eliminate cracking and to facilitate the trays slipping apart with ease. In addition, the trays are packed in foam and each one has an instruction label put on at the factory (because some customers couldn't figure out how to use the tray on their own). They still had occasional problems with cracking, especially during very cold weather, but the problems are limited. They always replace broken trays at no charge.

Distribution Of The Card-Well Tray

Initially the Cardwells went to local dealers to sell cases and quickly realized that they needed more widespread exposure. Then they ran an ad in *Sports Collectors Digest*—a trade magazine of card collecting. They got an immediate response from young boys, collectors and dealers who ordered the trays.

"Every time I got an order for a case, I would call every partner to share the good news," says Tammy. They got a call from a man in Washington who wanted to be their exclusive distributor for the West Coast, but they decided California was too big for one distributor. Thus, he accepted an exclusive for Washington, Oregon, Idaho, and Montana and has been one of their largest volume distributors.

Eventually the business started moving so fast that the Cardwells never seemed to stop working. Since all of the partners had full-time jobs, including Jack, Tammy took all the orders on her home computer, handled the bookkeeping, communicated with dealers, and did almost everything else, including shipping.

When people ask Tammy what it takes to have a successful business, she answers with tongue-in-cheek, "First you have to create a monster, then you have to feed the monster and, if you want it to flourish, be willing to live with it for the rest of your life."

She explains, "None of us realized the amount of work this business would take. We know now that all success demands a price, but we have also learned that you must get something out of it yourself, or you will start to resent the monster in a short period of time." Jack adds that the company has not become a monster because it does not control their lives. And, with no debt or overhead, the distributors keep selling the Card-Well trays—even in slow times.

Their home-based company, named "Goose Creek Enterprises," is a growing business. Although it doesn't support them with a full-time income, the Cardwells' goal is to be self-sufficient and Jack to be totally in business for himself. In the meantime, it has provided financial, physical, and emotional benefits. It started out as a sideline to pay for perks like baseball cards, tickets to Astro baseball games, and an occasional trip to a big card show in Atlanta that they otherwise couldn't afford.

And in the process of developing the product and growing the business, they see the benefits their own sons, Terry and Thomas, have gained from being involved: seeing firsthand how much work goes into running a business. "We have begun to grasp some business concepts and see how we're doing," says Jack.

Goose Creek Enterprises currently has seventeen distributors in the U.S., and two in Canada, Puerto Rico, and requests in Australia. But at this time it is too expensive to ship and pay customs "down under." (In each of the first three years of business, the company doubled its sales.)

SBA Publications For Developing
Ideas, Products, and Inventions

Can You Make Money With Your Idea or Invention? free
Ideas Into Dollars #P101, $2.00. Identifies the main challenges in product development and provides a list of resources to help inventors and innovators take their ideas into the marketplace.

Avoiding Patent, Trademark and Copyright Problems #P102, $2.00

Order all three booklets from SBA 1-800-827-5722

Factors That Contribute To Steady Growth

- *Aiming for top quality.* They do all they can to equate Goose Creek Enterprises and the Card-Well Tray with *Quality* at all times. "We have always felt it absolutely necessary to keep high standards, both in product quality and in service," says Tammy. It has always been their practice to replace damaged goods without questions, to ship quickly, and to not undercut their distributors in any way. They respond to people in a professional and expedient manner.

  On many occasions, they have seen the value of their stand on quality. Someone made a "Card-Well Copy," apparently taking their tray and duplicating it with a few minor changes. The "copy cat" then approached all of their distributors about marketing it for him. Each distributor called Jack and Tammy to say that he made it clear to the competitor that he was happy doing business with the Cardwells and wouldn't even consider changing.

- *Avoiding Debt.* By having investors and paying off half of them with interest within the first year and the others within the second year, Goose Creek Enterprises was able to avoid going into debt with bank loans. In the third year all partners were bought out and the business belonged solely to the Cardwells, its 800 number was paid for months in advance, and enough money was in the bank to build a new warehouse and operate on a cash basis for all transactions. And if the business were to completely shut down because of a slow baseball card market, they would have money in the bank and still own the products they had produced and owe no one.

- *Being Open to New Ideas and Constantly Getting Input and Counsel from Others.* "If someone says 'you could be doing it this way,' we're open to hear them. We've been blessed by fantastically helpful people," says Tammy. "Every week we are learning something. They also read a lot: books on time management, marketing, and business practices, and

131

listen to motivational tapes by Zig Ziglar and othe
speakers and business experts.

Thinking Creatively And Developing Your Ideas

Lots of people have ideas. But ideas are like beautiful butter-
flies we may watch hovering over a field of
flowers; they quickly blow away into the
wind, unless we catch them—either on
camera, with a net, or on canvas. We've got
to *do something* with the little brainstorms
and ideas we get. I love what John Steinbeck
said about handling ideas: "Ideas are like rabbits. You get a couple
and learn how to handle them, and pretty soon you have a dozen."

Think Creatively

Here are some ways to develop your creative ideas:

- Get an "IDEA" notebook and write down what you hope to
  do (i.e., start a business, solve a problem, create a new
  seminar or product)
- Using a clustering method of brainstorming (write your
  core idea or purpose in the center of the page and list
  around it like spokes around a wheel every single way you
  could achieve your goal)
- When ideas stop flowing, here's what one creative person I
  know does: "When my pen slows down and I can't think of
  anything else, I go play paddle tennis, drink a Snapple,
  walk my dog, or otherwise take a break and temporarily
  forget about what I'm brainstorming about." And that is
  often when the flash of insight or idea that you need hits
  you on the side of the head!
- Write it down—the new way to solve your problem, the creative
  idea—and now go through the steps to put it into action

Resources For Developing Your Creative Ideas

So You've Got a Great Idea, Steve Fiffer (NY: Addison-Wesley)

*A Whack on the Side of the Head: How to Unlock Your Mind for
Innovation,* von Oech

The Care and Feeding of Ideas by Bill Backer (NY: Random House)

A Fistful Of Advice For Pursuing Your Business Ideas

1. *Don't say, "I could never."* Tammy, who inherited a great "can-do" attitude from her family, has found what her mother said to be true that "Can't never could do nothin'!'" She was raised in an enterprising, hard-working family that operated, at different times: a janitorial business, a window-cleaning business, and later a business building custom-made fishing rods. The fishing rods developed into a full-fledged tackle store that still supports her mother today.

   "I had the opportunity to help in the businesses and had an active part in them. There was always a lot of work to do and everybody pitched in," she says. "I'm grateful because I learn so much and gained the attitude that if you decide to do something, it is possible, which gave me a feeling of worth."

   When her mom and dad had a problem to solve in the business, Tammy and her siblings were involved in the brainstorming for solutions. When she helped them find what they needed or came up with the solution, she felt important and knew what she had to say counted—a great self-esteem builder. Her suggestion to parents: put your children in the position of feeling worthwhile and contributing in some way to the household and business. In doing so, you boost their self-esteem and give them a sense of being needed and having potentil. A great idea worth following!

2. *Never assume you know it all.* Asking tons of questions (even if some seem stupid) is much better than making tons of mistakes. Asking questions is how scientists succeed in finding a cure and how people learn! Tammy and Jack Cardwell learned from plastics manufacturers, dealers who had purchased the trays, card collectors, foam distributors, baseball card store owners, and many other people who made suggestions and brainstormed with them on how to solve problems. They also learned from books and cassette tapes.

3. *Look before you leap.* This is great advice that *my* mom shared with me over and over in my growing-up years, but it certainly applies to starting a new business.

Consider all costs honestly for development of the idea, production, packing and shipping, advertising, etc. For instance, after much research, Jack found it would cost from $5,000 to $15,000 to tool the mold and produce the first trays for market. When enough money was raised, production started. However, they recently considered another product, but in examining the market and looking realistically at the costs, they decided not to risk money on a new item.

4. *Don't be selfish.* Always be ready to help others and remember that it is only when you give, that you receive.

5. *Keep your priorities straight.* To Jack and Tammy Cardwell, what's important is God, Family, and Business in that order. "One thing that I feel is vital in a home-based business is to know when to call it a day," Tammy says. "You can't have a family business, which is our goal for this one, if you don't have a family."

Since the Cardwells are a home-schooling family, managing family and business time is particularly important. Tammy has found the only way to juggle business, teaching her sons, and making a home is to:

- **Stay Organized:** She uses a three-ring notebook, in which she has her business "To Do" lists, personal and family calendar, home-schooling lesson plans, Christmas and birthday lists, a page for ideas, etc.

- Use quick-to-fix recipes for meals. Two good resources for making a month's worth of meals in a day is *Once-a-Month Cooking* (available from 1-800-A-FAMILY; Focus on the Family's resource number)

- Get the children involved in the housework. The Cardwells' older son cleans the kitchen and dining room; the other does the living room and washes towels. They both take care of their own room and laundry.

- Since Goose Creek Enterprises is strictly wholesale, they don't get inundated with calls, like a retail storefront. They are not tied to the phone from morning until night or on weekends. "We turn on the answering machine, which is absolutely necessary if you home school or have young children *and* run a business from home," she says. "And I have learned to live with unfinished business."

6. *Don't ever mix business and personal money.* Write yourself a check and give yourself a salary, but don't ever touch the business money for personal uses, or you can wind up with tax and serious financial problems that can cause you to go out of business.

7. *Handle Tax Matters Carefully.* Through keeping careful records and utilizing profits, the Cardwells were able to make property improvements, such as the warehouse in back of the house, and depreciate it (which provided further tax benefits). They also can deduct the office phone bill, the 800 number, transportation, deliveries, shipping, and other costs of the home-based business.

Record-keeping is essential for all mileage, phone calls and other tax deductibles. "Because many home-business tax deductions have been eliminated," says Jack, "it's not worth going into a home business just for the tax breaks. You must be pursuing your business for other reasons."

When asked how they have built a successful home and family business, this industrious couple says: "There is no special magic attached to us. The only real difference is that we believe that with God's help and hard work, there is nothing we can't do."

When Jack was recently laid off from his full-time job, in addition to marketing a nutritional product with a network marketing company, he began designing house plans and light commercial interior designs for small business offices as part of Goose Creek Enterprises,. The Card-Well tray continues to sell, although the market has declined in the past year; with their debt-freestanding, they will ride out the slow time and emerge with another great idea.

To contact Goose Creek Enterprises for information on the baseball card sorting Card-Well tray write:

Goose Creek Enterprises
P.O. Box 980
Baytown, TX 77522

For more information on building a prototype from an idea, protect and license your idea

*From Concept to Market,*Gary S. Lynn, New York, John Wiley & Sons, 1989.

13

Solve Your Problem and Help Others

The Story Of Healthy Exchanges

"When life handed me a lemon," says Joanna Lund, founder and President of Healthy Exchanges, "not only did I make it into healthy lemonade, I wrote the recipe down and later sold it!"

How Joanna Solved A Problem For Herself and Shared the Help With Others

On January 4, 1991 at 9:05 a.m. Joanna's third child left for the Persian Gulf War. After the goodbyes, Joanna got back into her car, not knowing if she would ever see her children again. Realizing their mortality made her look at her own. "I couldn't do anything for my kids except send care packages. But I could get healthier and handle the stress of the situation so they didn't get a call from Red Cross that their mom was in the hospital or had died. It was the least I could do on the homefront."

However, in order to do that, Joanna had a problem to solve. She was 46 years old and weighed in at 300 pounds after 28 frustrating years as a pro-dieter. With heart problems and diabetes rampant in her immediate family, and both parents having died an early death with heart complications, Joanna's health was on the edge. Her triglycerides were sky-high. She suffered from gout and other health problems.

An avowed stress-eater, Joanna knew she couldn't cope the way she always had—by reaching for cake donuts when she was worried about her children. "My kids were risking their lives overseas, and they didn't need their mother slowly killing herself at home with food."

That day Joanna decided to get off the diet rollercoaster and start living healthy. Her story is a good example of one who *first* solved a problem for herself and then went on to help others—creating a thriving, phenomenally successful home business in the process.

From Kitchen Hobby To Business

Joanna's quest for good-tasting "common-folk" dishes led her to begin experimenting with all types of recipes prepared with low fat, low sugar and low sodium. She recalls, "I was looking for foods that were healthy enough for me and tasty enough for my truck-driving husband."

Time was short. Joanna had a full-time job as a commercial life underwriter in the day and carried twelve hours of college courses at night. Thus, she needed recipes that were quick to prepare and contained ingredients available in the small town grocery store in DeWitt (population 4500), Iowa.

The first recipe she created, Mexicali Pie, went to work in her brown bag the next day as a leftover lunch. "When I started taking my healthy food to work, people started picking on my plate. So I started bringing two lunches, one for me and one for the samplers." Every day her co-workers wanted the recipes, so Joanna wrote them down and kept the copy machine busy printing them. One of her co-workers said, "I love your recipes. My husband will eat them and my finicky daughter likes them. Why don't you put them together and write a cookbook?"

That idea lit another fire under Joanna, for by now she had created several hundred recipes which she catagorized (and already lost 60 pounds). Then she created more good-tasting, healthy dishes. Those first months of steady work in her small kitchen using co-workers and family as "diet food testers," led to her first cookbook, *Healthy Exchanges,* which was self-published in 1991.

Self-Publishing: A Step of Faith

Joanna continued creating recipes and asked a friend to do the artwork on the cookbook. That summer, after all three of her children had returned safely from the Persian Gulf and were back in the States, she began looking for a printer to produce 200 cookbooks for her family, friends, and neighbors. Since printing costs decreased with quantity, Joanna ordered 1,000.

"Since I had little money after paying the phone company for calls to and from my kids during the Persian Gulf War, I borrowed $2,000 to start the printing of the cookbooks," said Joanna. "My husband's words ring in my ears, 'I sure hope you know what you're doing or we're going to be paying for cookbooks for a long time.'"

After the first 150 were given away, Joanna had 750 cookbooks left to sell. So she began contacting radio and TV stations to let people know about them. Her sales promotion worked: all 1,000 books were gone in a month. She paid the bank off and went back to the printer for more books.

"By the fall of 1991 I'd lost almost 100 pounds. I had more weight to lose and more recipes inside my head, and I hadn't ever seen a food newsletter."

At that point Joanna decided to start a food newsletter and started telling people about her product. Two hundred-three people signed up for a year's subscription—sight unseen. Joanna wrote it, her printer printed it, and in just three and a half years she now has over 15,000 subscribers.

Joanna also self-published two more cookbooks, and has sold 200,000 copies of them herself, including her latest book, the *Health Wagon Journal,* her "Manual for Real World Living" in which she shares her secrets of healthy food, moderate exercise and positive attitude. She has also added a motivational audio tape, booklet, videotape, and line of seasonings to her product.

By January, 1995, just four years after her healthy lifestyle began, Joanna has left more than 130 pounds behind (and her insurance job) and gained "Healthy Exchanges" as a full-time career. Joanna does the creating, marketing, correspondence and mailing of products. She writes the newsletter and cookbooks, and has spoken to over 15,000 people in the past three years in addition to doing radio and television interviews—but not all by herself! She employs 14 people, including husband Cliff (business manager and director of sales) to keep up with the day-to-day pace of the business. A big room, the size of a two-car garage, was built on to their small bungalow for an office.

Self-Publishing Tips

- Select the right topic, one that you have expertise and one that meets the felt needs of your prospective readers. (Earning money, self-improvement and self-help are two of the top subjects for successful self-published books.)
- Check out the prices, services, and printing products of several printers to determine which is best for your budget and publishing needs. Offset printing and photocopying are two alternatives; photocopying being the least expensive. With the improvements in technology at "quick-print" shops, the quality of photocopying has improved tremendously. For reproducing of photographs or using color, offset printing is preferable.
- To market your book or booklet: write and send out a Press Release to local newspapers; sell your book at a discount to local bookstores; use direct mail and classified ads.

Love . . . Not Just Money

Does it sound like Joanna is working at her home business 24 hours a day with no time to stop? Does it sound like she's created a monster? Not so. "I love what I'm doing, so therefore, it's not work." (Although she adds they do try very hard to leave Sunday as a day of rest, recreation, and family time.)

Resource for Self-Publishing:

The Self-Publishing Manual—How to Write, Print, and Sell Your Own Book, Dan Poynter, Para Publishing, P. O. Box 4232-O, Santa Barbara, CA 93140

Managing Your Time The Healthy Exchange Way

How does Joanna have the energy to do everything she's doing and still stay cheerful, enthusiastic, and *married?* "I get up between 3:30 and 4:30 a.m. and take care of my 'first things': praying and meditating, creative thinking, and computer work," she says. By 7:00 a.m. she is ready to go to the local health club for water aerobics, walk for 45 minutes on the country roads near their home, or ride to town on a bicycle for her errands. "I put on five to six miles a day on my bicycle doing errands such as going to the post office and grocery store." By 9:00 p.m. she is asleep, unless she is out at a speaking engagement.

Joanna seems to have more energy than many 24-year-olds. She has so much to share that she never runs out of enthusiasm: "My purpose on earth is to share my commonsense approach to eating and living, my healthy recipes, and to help people accept their bodies as God created them. We're not all created to have movie-star figures."

If bad weather prevents her outdoor exercise, she "walks the house" non-stop for 20 minutes to music. If she and Cliff are on the road for speaking, she walks the mall. "Once a day we pull into a mall, check the bookstores inside to see if they have my books, and get good exercise."

Mothering First

"If my kids were still little and at home, I wouldn't be speaking 30 times in 35 days. My mother responsibilities came first. But my children are now grown. There's a time and place for everything in the seasons of our lives. A home business is ideal for mothers at home, but you can't give it full throttle until your children are older."

You can profit from Joanna's best advice: Whatever home business you embark on, go into it for the love of it, not just money. Don't look at the top money-maker businesses and pursue one of them if your heart isn't in it. Look at what you *love* to do that you could turn into a business.

You're going to be committing a lot of time to it, and so is your family. You need to genuinely love and nurture it. "Don't go after the big bucks," admonishes Joanna. "If you truly love what you're doing and are doing it in a way that uses your God-given talents to the maximum as He intended, the money will follow—maybe not Cadillac money but Chevy money!"

- **The Golden Rule:**
  "My one unwritten rule in business is to treat everyone the way I would want to be treated—employees, customers, business associates. I always think, if I were on the other side, how would I want to be treated?"

More Secrets of Success

- **The Five-a-Week Rule:**
  Joanna applies the USDA's "Five-A-Day" Principle (five fruits and vegetables) to her home business and aims to let *five new people in the media,* one each day of the week, know about Healthy Exchanges. How does she accomplish this goal?
  "I call, I write. It could be a radio talk-interview I do at home via telephone, or a TV station in an area where I'm speaking." Multiply that five contacts a week times 52 weeks a year and you have a grassroots movement!

When you do make contacts with media, send a press kit which contains:

Do-It-Yourself Press Kit

- Name of your organization, phone, fax, e-mail address, etc.
- Business card attached to front pocket
- A news release, or latest press release
- A publicity calendar of upcoming events and speaking engagements
- A fact sheet (can be used instead of a press release)

- A background sheet
- Quotes sheet with recommendations on your services, books, or products
- Copies of previously printed news articles or feature stories about you and your business
- Brochure if it has information connected to the announcement, or copies of your newsletter if you publish one, or latest book
- A publicity photo, usually 5" X 7" black and white
- A "Bio," concise biographical sheet which can be called "About the Author"

Put the above contents in a folder with interior pockets.

Once a month Joanna picks a spot out on the map and tells her husband "This is where I want to go." It might be a new area or an area where she has a cooking demonstration to conduct. She books herself to and from the region in cities and towns along the way.

With her *Five-A-Week* principle which has produced hundreds of interviews and speaking engagements, and word-of-mouth spreading the message, Healthy Exchanges has experienced phenomenal growth in just three and a half years. The circle of her speaking engagements keeps growing and growing. She donates a portion of every speaker's fee to "Camp Courageous" in Iowa, a camp for the physically and mentally handicapped.

Promoting Your Business By Speaking

As Joanna did, you can promote your business, service, or product by speaking before professional and civic groups in your community, (and eventually state and nation-wide). Organizations and groups are continually needing speakers for their luncheons, conventions, and other events. With more than 9,000 speaking opportunities each day in the U.S.,[7] there are ample chances for terrific promotional possibilities for home-based business owners.

- Create a flyer or brochure with your credentials, speaking credits, and suggested topics. Add short recommendations from past speaking engagements

- Mail your materials promoting your speaking with a business card to the groups, organizations, and businesses that would be interested in your area of expertise.

- Offer to speak free for "practice" as many times as it takes for you to feel confident with your topics, and polish your communication techniques

- When possible, take along to speaking engagements a friend or associate who has a background in oral communications or drama who can critique your presentation (voice, posture, diction, and techniques) and offer suggestions for improvement

- Read books and listen to audio tapes by successful speakers such as Zig Ziglar for tricks and techniques of the trade such as using audio-visual aids, creating handouts for the audience, etc. Whenever a renowned or popular speaker is in town, go hear him or her and take notes!

- Arrange in advance to have a book table following the event where you are speaking. Sell your books, tapes, booklets, and include free brochures about your services and products.

Resources for Speakers

Speaking With Confidence: A Guide for Public Speakers,
Wanda Vassallo, White Hall, Virginia,
Betterway Publications, Inc. 1990

Speak and Grow Rich, Dottie and Lillie Walters,
Englewood Cliffs, NJ, 1989

The Quick and Easy Way to Effective Speaking, Dale Carnegie,
a classic on speaking with success (Pocket Books, Dept. of DCR,
1230 Avenue of the Americas, New York, NY 10020)

Speaker's Desk Book of Quips, Quotes and Anecdotes, Jacob M. Braude,
Englewood Cliffs, NJ: Prentice-Hall, Inc., 1963

Besides her speaking, Joanna's "velvet hammer approach" has contributed to the success of the business: letting people know about Healthy Exchanges, but not hounding them to death with it. "You have to be willing to talk about what you're doing. You can see whether the person's eyes glaze over or sparkle with interest.

You have to know how to market your product or service, whether it's a fantastic loaf of bread to a cookbook—no matter how good it is. People have got to know about it to buy it," Joanna adds.

Good News for Healthy Exchange

Joanna's publicity and marketing campaign is paying off: several large New York City publishers discovered her cookbooks, and she has agreed to write two new books for Putnam & Sons Publishing. The first was released Spring of 1995, and was already accepted even before publication as a selection by *Prevention* and *Better Homes and Gardens* book clubs, and as an alternate selection for the Doubleday Health book club. Her second book will be released in 1996. "I have a wonderful food editor," says Joanna. Putnam editors encouraged her to continue writing in her "Grandma Moses" style, which she defines as "professional enough to be accepted by the professionals but soft and gentle enough to be understood by anyone with a sixth grade education."

She has recently been appointed to the President's White House Council on Small Business representing Iowa and has been appointed by the Governor to his special commission on rural health. "All this because I quit dieting and started living healthy and showing others how to do the same!" says Joanna.

14

On the Cutting Edge: Starting a Service Business

How would you like to operate a business which is flexible, mobile, enables you to keep family first, yet produces regular income and enables you to really help people and make a difference in their lives?

That's what Nancy O'Donnell, an Oklahoma City mother of three, was looking for when her three girls were in school—and she found it in "The Cutting Edge," her knife and scissor-sharpening service business. From the beginning, Nancy's desire was to work only two days a week. So she arranged her schedule to making service calls on Tuesday and Thursdays. Her workday started when her daughters caught the bus for school, and ended before school was out. Thus, Nancy was available for a chat and snack with her daughters or to drive them to extracurricular activities.

"Family is my top priority at this time of my life," says Nancy, who pursued a number of hobbies she thoroughly enjoyed, and wanted time to continue quilting, flower and vegetable gardening, and creative cooking. The flexible schedule of her service business met all the criteria and filled her need for extra income. It also provided her a wonderful opportunity to develop relationships with many of her customers and help them.

Service Businesses: The Growth Industry Of The '90s

Experts agree that service businesses will be the most successful businesses of not only this decade, but also of the 21st century. Because of the fast pace of this information age where life is speeded up into fast forward both at work and home, new gaps are opened that can be filled up by *service*. Many lucrative service businesses are begun by someone doing what others don't have time to do, or want to do. It may be a business that leaves one more leisure or family time. Whether it is house or office cleaning, tax consulting, apartment finding, or express mail, service businesses help make life manageable for people.

That point leads to the benefits of service businesses: Besides the flexibility and independence of owning your own business, service enterprises give you the opportunity to touch people's lives and build relationships. If you enjoy serving others and working with people, service may be just the niche for you. Our society relies more and more on services, so the opportunities grow every day.

Where Did the Sharpening Service Idea Come From?

In Nancy's case, she had heard about a friend of her husband who had developed a very successful knife-sharpening business on the East Coast. It sounded just like what she'd like to tackle—with the flexibility, time investment, and small start-up capital requirements that fit her budget and lifestyle.

Before beginning the business, she did her "homework." Nancy talked to the East Coast sharpener at length to get details and tips on starting this type of service business. She researched what supplies she would need to purchase in order to begin and where to learn how to sharpen tools properly. Owners of a knife shop in the city were happy to demonstrate correct sharpening skills. Not only were they glad to train her; they were thrilled that she was going to be "mobile." They often received calls from restaurants and individuals requesting that a service person come to their kitchen or business site to sharpen tools. Since they simply could not provide mobile service, they promised to refer all mobile business to her.

In addition, shortly after Nancy began her sharpening service, a man called who had been in the business for many years. He offered to teach her how to sharpen scissors and garden tools. With her education complete, she began to look at start-up costs.

> ### Service Business Checklist

Before going into business here are some necessary steps to lay the groundwork and do basic business planning:

❏ Choose your service business and name

❏ Design company logo to match your philosophy and purpose

❏ Count the Cost: Figure all start-up costs. (And avoid taking on a large debt.)

❏ Figure the fee you will need to charge. As in pricing products, your fee (which depends in part on your skill and experience) should be high enough to cover your overhead and expenses, enable you to make a profit, yet reasonable enough to attract and keep customers in line with your competition. For a mobile service business as "The Cutting Edge," equipment and gasoline expenses should be figured in. Check with other similar services for pricing information. (Nancy decided on an hourly rate.)

❏ Figure out and list how you will advertise and find customers.

What to Do Next

Write a target date beside each one of the above tasks to be completed. Check each one off as you accomplish it. Business planning, even in the basics above, pushes you to map out your business, set income goals, consider working capital, etc. Just as a writer composes an entire proposal with chapter outlines and the whole concept of the book before beginning or presenting the idea to a publisher, just as a builder begins with a blueprint before constructing a house, *you need a plan before starting your business.*

Service Business: A Golden Opportunity

Like other service businesses, this particular business was a golden opportunity for an entrepreneur like Nancy, because the start-up costs were lower than for wholesale, retail, or manufacturing businesses. With motivation, resourcefulness, and a limited budget, Nancy launched "The Cutting Edge."

The initial investment was less than $400 for all tools, equipment, and business cards with the logo, "The Cutting Edge." Nancy's dad built a small table to fit in her mini-van to sharpen the tools on-site. Nancy decided to operate the sharpening service for six weeks on a trial basis. In two months she had made her investment back, and the business has continued to steadily grow every since.

Now, after six and a half years, "The Cutting Edge" has expanded so much that Nancy has regular clients every month and season of the year (with spring being the busiest time for sharpening gardening tools and the fall months the busiest months for sharpening knives and scissors). At the beginning of each month, Nancy pulls out cards on which she has all her appointments lined up for the next thirty days.

How Does Your Business Grow: Finding Customers

In any service business, one first must identify and contact potential customers. Nancy began this process by notifying friends that she was offering a knife-sharpening service. She gave each friend her business card. They became her first satisfied customers. They told their friends about her service, who told their friends. . . and so "The Cutting Edge" grew, by word-of-mouth, the best advertising of all.

Nancy has never gone door-to-door. Her business has expanded from referrals, although there are many ways to advertise a service business. Eighty-five to ninety percent of Nancy's business is residential; the rest of her accounts are large, national-chain restaurants in the city. Although she never went after commercial business, they called her because they had a need for her services. Her best marketing tool was satisfied customers who spread the word.

How to Find Clients

- Newspaper advertising (smaller community newspapers and weekly newspapers offer the cheapest prices for ads)
- Yellow Pages of the phone directory
- Flyer announcing your service business: Display on grocery store bulletin board, church or community center bulletin board

Promoting Your Service Business

- Send flyer and/or business card to a mailing list of friends and people likely to need your service
- Offer to write article for local newspaper on how to sharpen tools(or whatever your service provides); tie your article in to the current season (Christmas—knife-sharpening, summer—gardening, etc.)
- Offer a free demonstration at a shop, or for a local club meeting—this approach is not only good public relations; you will meet many potential customers
- Encourage and reward word-of-mouth references

Satisfied Customers: Your Best Marketing Tool

"This service is so unique because many people don't know where to take their tools to be sharpened, or it is a big hassle to drive across town and leave them for a few days—especially if you are a restaurant owner," says Nancy. "The Cutting Edge" is also distinctive in that she is the only woman sharpener in the large metroplex area, and the only such service that is mobile.

Living by the Golden Rule—treating others the way you would like to be treated—means that you have to be willing to treat people better than they may be willing to treat you.
—Michael Josephson

"People love the convenience," she adds. "I'm constantly getting referrals. This is a wonderful business for a woman." Women feel quite comfortable about having Nancy in their home to check their knives, scissors, and tools. Since she takes everything to her van to sharpen, there is no mess or noise for the customer, and all tools are returned to them, cleaned, sharpened, and ready to use—within the hour.

The customer sees immediate results. Her clients also appreciate the fact that Nancy follows up, keeps detailed notes on the condition of their tools, and calls for a maintenance appointment on the date they indicated, depending on their needs. Some customers like her to come by once a year; many every six months. A few gourmet cooks and restaurants ask for service every three or four months. (*Consumer Reports* magazine recommends sharpening knives and scissors *at least once a year.*)

Possible Service Businesses

Look at the needs of people in your community—where is there a gap you could fill? Then look at your skills, past experience, and talents to find a good match. Know what the customer wants and then brainstorm—how can I provide it better than the competitors?

Service Businesses Worth Starting

- Swimming pool maintenance
- Lawncare; landscaping
- Catering business
- Mobile Dog Grooming Service
- Medical transcription service
- Janitorial services: house and office cleaning; window cleaning
- Organizing services: closets, offices, kitchens, garage sales
- Shopping service
- Clown service for birthday parties and school carnivals
- In-home postpartum care service
- Golf club repair (or bicycle, lawn mower, or electronics)
- Dressmaking/alterations
- Framing pictures
- Computer services; computer consulting

- Photography service: portraits, weddings, in-studio and on-location
- Childcare
- Shuttle service for working moms for their kids' after-school activities
- Apartment-finding service

Golden Service: The Secret to Nancy's Success

Service businesses are people-oriented. If you love working with people, you'll likely enjoy a service business. And relationship-building is one of the keys to success.

"When I started my own business, I wanted to treat my customers the way I wanted to be treated by service-based people—the first factor was punctuality," says Nancy, who is extremely punctual. In that rare instance when she is late (even fifteen minutes), Nancy calls her client to inform them. She also makes a habit of contacting each client the night before the scheduled appointment to confirm the time. "Many people have to wait all day for servicemen, but not my customers!" she adds.

The next priority for Nancy was to be fair and honest with people. She treats her customers with the utmost kindness and goes overboard to please. She guarantees all work. If she sharpens a pair of scissors, for example, and after the process they won't cut an eighth inch at the tip, she doesn't charge. She may even recommend that they be thrown away if they are defective or worn out.

"It's essential to me to deal with people upfront and honestly, even if it means not making money on one appointment." Sometimes she finds customers have been charged outlandish prices and their knives still aren't sharp or the scissors won't work. But not Nancy's clients. They trust her to go in and check their equipment and to sharpen only the tools that need it. "I know immediately if a tool is worn out, and I won't charge for that," says Nancy.

How can you take the philosophy of this service business and apply it to whatever service business you go into? Based on your philosophy of business and the concept or service you provide, list the three ways you will treat your customers to deliver "golden service":

PEOPLE-SKILLS

1.

2.

3.

When Nancy goes to a client's house, she first looks over all the equipment and offers a few hints about maintaining tools, whether kitchen, sewing, or garden tools. (Example: avoid putting knives in the dishwasher. The combined damage of heat and water pressure cause the knives to hit against dishes and pans and results in little knicks. Knives last a lot longer if handwashed.)

After sharpening, she may suggest the best place to store knives, and oils the handles of wooden tools to preserve them. The average appointment lasts one hour. However, as she has become more experienced ("I've sharpened literally thousands and thousands of knives and scissors," she says) she is faster and has streamlined her methods.

Service Business is Friendship-Business

One of the aspects Nancy enjoys most about her business is the opportunity to meet so many people and to touch their lives. "Service is the most people-oriented of all business," says Ben Chant in *How to Start a Service Business*. All service businesses have this one factor in common—regular interaction with others. Since "people skill" is one of Nancy's gifts, it's a good match.

"I've met some wonderful people doing this and have made some great friends," Nancy adds. "I wouldn't trade the business—and the friends I've made—for anything." A service business like "The Cutting Edge" is in some ways a mission; Nancy runs into people who are lonely, who share personal things with her, who just need an encouraging word. She likes to bring in new people and continue to build up her business as customers are referred to her.

Occasional promotions at local fabric shops enlarge Nancy's customer base. She also does demonstrations and promotions at the Classic Gourmet, a kitchen and cooking shop where she met several new clients.

Best Advice From a Sharp Businesswoman

If this type of business sounds like a good idea to you, put into practice some of the great advice below. And if sharpening knives and tools is not your cup of tea, you can apply the principles to just about any service business:

- *Don't get discouraged.* It takes time to build your service business. Referrals (i.e., when your service is recommended to your customer's close friend) take more time, but you will get better customers in the long run. It took Nancy almost five years to build her business and expand it to the point that at the beginning of each month, all her appointments are filled with regular, repeat customers.

- *Be organized!* You will need a good filing system to keep all your customer records on. Organization is the key to your personal customer service. Nancy designed her own organization system to fit "The Cutting Edge": she has a card for each customer, on which she makes notes at appointments: which knives or tools she sharpens; the condition of the knives and tools; the date the customer wants her to return for a service call. These cards are color-coded. The town adjoining, Edmond, is yellow; a

Carry Your Business Cards Everywhere You Go, and Especially on Customer Calls. Give One to Each Customer, and Leave a Few Extras For Friends Who Might Need Your Service.

neighborhood where she has many clients, Nichols Hills, is green. This way, she plans her days so that she is in one area all day making appointments, which saves driving time and expense.

You also need to keep excellent records for auto mileage, taxes, and all business expenses.

- *Get excellent equipment.* Fine equipment is essential to doing quality sharpening, and it is a small investment overall. A grinder and a few basic tools can be purchased and paid for in a few months of work.

- *Get good training.* Talk to the owners of sharpening shops in your area for names of experienced people who could teach you the skills you need. Good training on *scissor sharpening* is especially important. "Scissors can be your biggest money-maker, but scissors are the easiest tools to ruin if you don't know the proper way to sharpen them," Nancy says.

Sideline to Service—Great Idea for a Line of Products

A perfect adjunct to a service business like this one is a line of high-quality knives, scissors, and garden tools to sell to your customers. Just as beauty operators do a brisk side business selling hair and nail products, people would often rather buy related products from a trusted service person who they know is an expert on quality tools or products in his area of service.

The beauty of the service industry and of a service business like "The Cutting Edge" lies in its simplicity and low start-up costs. I hope this chapter has helped you get a "grip" on the benefits of service businesses, given you creative ideas, or filled in a few pieces of the puzzle you needed to start the service-oriented business of your dreams. If you have questions concerning the O'Donnell filing and organization system, or the sharpening business, write to her for more information and be sure to send a self-addressed stamped envelope to:

The Cutting Edge,
11004 N. St. Charles,
Oklahoma City, OK 73162.

Suggested Resources

How to Start a Service Business, Ben Chant and Melissa Morgan
(NY: Avon, 1994)

Consumer Reports Magazine; available at public libraries and
bookstores

How to Advertise: A Handbook for the Small Business,
Sandra L. Dean (Dearborn, 1983)

Finding Your Niche . . . Marketing Your Professional Service,
Bart Brodsky and Janet Geis; The New Careers Center, Inc.;
P. O. Box 339-CT; Boulder, CO 80306

Budgeting in a Small Service Firm,
SBA publication #FM08 (1-800-827-5722)

Business Plan Small for Service Firms,
SBA publication #MP11 (1-800-827-5722)

15

Dollars and "Sense"

Nancraft: Professional Crafter and Consultant

"I never started out in life to go in this direction," says Nancy Mosher, writer and former teacher. "The magazines I write for would be a surprise to my high school English teacher who said, 'You can't write, Nancy.'"

Twenty-five years ago Nancy began making crafts as a hobby and sewing (alterations and dressmaking) as a home-based business. Actually, she had been making crafts for most of her life. By the second year of her marriage, the Mosher Christmas tree was filled with only handmade ornaments, and Nancy delighted friends and family with handmade gifts for birthdays, Christmas, and other occasions.

Tole painting, quilling, needlepoint, clay sculpture, decoupage, and macrame are just a few of the crafts and techniques that Nancy pursues. Once she learns the basics, she uses her creativity by designing her own projects. She also enjoys teaching others and has written and published two craft books, *Chenille Show Offs* (1973) and *Quill-a-Way Christmas* (1975) she wrote and had published.

Nancy has taught crafts to adults in Community education programs, children's craft classes at home, and even developed a series of classes for Scout leaders and school teachers called "Projects for Pennies."

In the late '70s Nancy became a professional "crafter," selling her products at many of the local craft shows in Kansas, Oklahoma, and beyond. When craft malls began to open up, Nancy began renting booth space and found success selling there as well.

By meeting crafters at shows, stores, and her own classes, Nancy discovered that many professional crafters were deficient in the bookkeeping area of their business. She explains, "Most do not have a business background. They like to create and see other people's work selling at fairs and shows. So they start creating without a solid foundation. A friend encourages, 'You should make and sell them . . .' and off they go."

Nancy came to the conclusion that without a bookkeeping system or basic business practice, the majority of crafters didn't make it. They weren't making money and couldn't meet expenses at a craft show. Nancy saw an urgent need for bookkeeping information, and began presenting business-management seminars and writing articles for craft magazines.

3 Pitfalls of the Professional Crafter

1. Beginning crafters think crafts are an easy way to make pocket money.
2. The only time many crafters do their bookkeeping is at income tax time.
3. Crafters tend to co-mingle their business and personal money.

Best Advice for the Crafter

If you start out in the right direction by applying the principles below, or if you are already crafting and selling, make the suggested adjustments and you'll reap huge benefits in your business.

Success is not a matter of luck or genius. Success depends on adequate preparation and indomitable determination.

—Anonymous

If you are interested in making and selling crafts, attend craft shows and read magazines. Go to department and gift stores to observe the colors, trends, and mood of what's out there and what's selling. Would your products fit or are they so outdated or different that they won't sell? "Different can be good if there's a niche for it," says Nancy. Beginning crafters often have poor quality and price their product too high. It helps to get a big picture of the inventory currently in shops.

First, test market a few items in small craft shows where you can have a table rather than rent an expensive booth. At many church and hospital auxiliaries, holiday bazaars or town festivals you can exhibit for as little as $10.

Take a craft course or two that teaches you techniques and lets you begin networking with other crafters. The methods and techniques you learn can be a springboard to using your own creativity. "Don't be a copycat," says Nan. "Have the courage to design your own creations. But keep abreast of the changing trends—especially in color."

Make your crafts enterprise legitimate: register your business name at the appropriate city office. Get a resale tax number and any other registration necessary in your community or state—which brings up the matter of expert advice: Hire a CPA to do your income taxes, and he/she can advise you on what you need to do to legitimatize your business.

Have a business card made up. Money spent on business cards will reap rewards in the end. Your image and professionalism in communicating with the rest of the business world, the craft industry, and your customers, can be a big factor in the success or failure of your business.

Buy your equipment and raw materials for your finished goods (such as glue gun, paints, ribbon, dried and silk flowers, fabric, etc.) at the lowest possible price you can find without compromising quality. To do this, you will need a retail tax number. "Many crafters avoid the tax part, so they pay retail price for their materials, with the sales tax built on it. Then, when they sell the item they end up paying sales tax twice." With a tax number, even if you need to purchase some items at a retail store, they waive sales tax on raw materials. When you sell it, you pay sales tax *once* instead of twice. Check with your State Tax Commission for the application you need to file for a tax number.

Dollars and "Sense": Setting Up Your Bookkeeping System

Set up a good bookkeeping system from the beginning so that if asked, you could get out your ledger and tell them how much you spent and grossed to date. "Only five out of fifty crafters have any idea about that vital information," reports Nancy. Most use the "Shoebox" method of bookkeeping in which they throw all receipts and bills in a shoebox and the only time they worry about bookkeeping is at tax time. They have no business checking account and may not be paying sales tax, she adds. This is a sure recipe for disaster.

Bookkeeping for Crafters

- *Open a business checking account* which you only use for business expenses.

- *Have an Income Ledger and an Expense Ledger,* on separate pages, to record all financial transactions. Nancy recommends a 14 column ledger sheet page with room for many categories. **Money coming in** is recorded on sales slips, receipts, invoices, or deposit slips. *Money going out* is usually recorded in your checkbook or in receipts for cash purchases.

- *Keep separate categories for your expenses.* Expenses include raw materials and equipment, advertising expenses, travel expenses, broken down (see Sidebar on "Crafter's Travel Tips") booth rent, long-distance phone charges, crafter magazines and books (resources), office supplies, and any other expenses you incur in making and selling your crafts.

- *Keep all receipts, deposit slips, and invoices. Then close out your books at the end of each month* and figure up how much you spent and made. Clip these receipts together and write a summary profit-and-loss statement on the front with the month and year. (To get the amount of your profit or loss subtract your total expenses from the total receipts to date.)

File this financial information in a folder or big envelope, and it becomes part of your permanent tax record. If you are ever audited, you have the proof of your business transactions. Knowing if you are making or losing money is also very important for making sound business decisions about whether to travel to a craft show out-of-state, develop a new product, or invest in a piece of equipment.

By doing bookkeeping, and closing out books each month, you will have all 12 months done when tax time comes. You will reduce your costs of tax preparation from your CPA. You will also have less chance of losing a receipt and not being able to get the deduction. "Take every deduction when you have spent money on your business," says Nancy. But be sure to keep documentation of the expense, or you can't take it as a business deduction.

Nancy finds her relationship with a professional accountant helpful, not only for filing taxes, but for informing her of new tax laws that affect her home-based business. She would much rather call and say, "Hi, Joe, what do I have to do differently in my record-keeping this year?" or "How have the laws changed and how is it going to affect my business this year?" than have to read the books on the new tax laws and deductions. That way she can spend her time doing what she loves best: crafting and creating, teaching and helping other people.

"Shop for an accountant just as carefully as you would for a dentist, doctor, or a car," advises Nancy. She suggests finding a CPA that has expertise in home-based businesses and knows about crafting. A big corporate lawyer or divorce lawyer doesn't know the deductions and tax details for home-based businesses.

- *Don't mingle craft money and personal money.* In other words, don't spend grocery money for craft supplies and don't spend the craft mall pay check on a pair of shoes for your child. Keep the two separate and you will save yourself a lot of stress and confused records! With separate checking

163

accounts you can avoid the temptation. Then, write a check out of the business account to pay yourself a "salary" which you deposit in your personal account.

Travel Tips for The Crafter

It's the little things that get lost. This can be true for travel expense receipts. Create a positive habit of keeping track so that receipts will not get lost. Here's how Nancy does this:

- Before each business trip, get a letter size envelope, and write on the outside the location, date, and reason for the trip.

- Put the envelope in a convenient place: vehicle sunvisor pocket or purse. Then instead of stuffing the receipt just any old place there is always *that one place* to put it.

- Travel expense receipts include meals, motel, parking and toll road fees. Even emergency craft supply or display purchase receipt can be put in the envelope.

- With the receipts together in the envelope, it will then be an easy job to record all your travel expenses into the bookkeeping ledger upon returning home.

If you do sell your crafts at a craft mall, look at different malls first to match up your needs and the craft mall needs. "A craft mall is just like a small retail store, but you don't have to be there every day," says Nancy. She has her products in two malls in the Dallas metroplex area. To succeed in a craft mall you must be unique and have high-quality products, good prices, and an orderly booth.

"If you don't want to deal with customers or be tied to retail hours, try renting a craft mall booth," encourages Nancy. "The rent is considerably less than an individual storefront location, and the craft mall is manned by one or several salespeople who sell merchandise from the different booths. However, you need to regularly straighten your crafts or gift items to make sure the displays are attractive and neat. Mall customers are constantly handling and rearranging your products and displays in a way you hadn't planned. For successful craft mall sales, keep up with market trends and *continue developing ideas* for successful craft mall sales.

Don't be afraid to change your prices, and always consider your labor and overhead in the price of the product.

Read, Read, Read! Read books and trade magazines to keep up with the latest news about craft and home-based businesses. Some recommended ones are listed below.

Resources for the Crafter—Books

Homemade Money, Creative Cash, Barbara Brabec Productions
P. O. Box 2137, Naperville, IL 60567

How to Profit From Your Crafts, Income Opportunities Manuals
P. O. Box 40, Vernon, NJ 07462

Trade Journals for the Crafter

The Crafts Report
P. O. Box 1992
Wilmington, Delaware 19899

Craft Supply Magazine
225 Gordons Corner Road
Manalapan, NJ 07726

Arts and Crafts ShowGuide
ACN Publications
P. O. Box 104628
Jefferson City, MO 65110-4628

Neighbors and Friends
P. O. Box 294403
Lewisville, TX 75057-4402

Helping the Crafter
Become Accepted by the Craft Industry

As in most industries and businesses, the craft industry has trade shows. Manufacturers and distributors of craft supplies, plus retail store owners, publishers, and others interested in craft supplies attend these shows. Trade shows also include technique classes and educational seminars which provide opportunities to network with others in the industry.

For many years the professional crafter has not been well

accepted at the trade shows. "Often the crafter has been considered the poor step-child of the craft industry," Nancy says. Crafters often do not know how to work with manufacturers and sales reps. Thus, many industry exhibitors at trade shows prefer that crafters not attend.

However, recently the trade organizations began to realize that the Professional Crafter category was the fastest growing segment of the craft industry. Thus, Nancy Mosher, being a veteran professional crafter, seminar teacher, and former craft store employee, was asked to become a board member of two organizations in the craft industry. She is the first crafter to ever serve on their boards.

Nancy's mission, while serving on the Board of Directors of the Association of Craft and Creative Industries (ACCI) and the Southwestern Craft & Hobby Association (ACCI), is to help the professional crafter become an integral part of the craft industry.

Building Integrity as a Professional Crafter

Perhaps you are like many crafters and home-based business entrepreneurs who want to live the American dream "to be your own boss." As Nancy says, "Sorry folks, but even self-employed people have bosses!" Maybe not in the strictest sense of the word, but because of an agreement or a commitment, as a crafter or businessperson, you have responsibilities to someone else, whether short or long term. (In the dictionary the word "boss" is described as an employer, supervisor, person who makes decisions; to manage, direct, control.)

In other words, there are responsibilities that you as a business person are obligated to fulfill. Your business's credibility and reputation is built in part by meeting these obligations.

The Crafter's "Boss"

Craft Mall Manager

When you sign a craft mall agreement or lease, you take on certain obligations which could include: paying rent on time, staying for full term of the agreement, adhering to the description of the items that can or cannot be sold, and honoring special orders that the store has taken in your behalf. The mall also has certain obligations to you, and you expect them to be honored.

Craft Show Promotor/Coordinator

A short-term boss, the craft show coordinator and you have made an agreement. As a crafter, you take on the responsibiity of paying the booth fees on time, keeping the booth display within prescribed dimensions, selling only the crafts outlined in the agreement, fulfilling special orders, and staying until the end of the show's selling period.

Buyers of special orders

Any free-lance special order you take comes from a "boss." It is your responsibility to see that the order is completed and delivered to the buyer in a timely manner and to the agreed-upon specifications.

Craft Supply Distributor:

When the crafter sets up an account or financial relationship with a craft supply distributor, you strive to get an open account as a means of buying. An open account comes with several requirements: the maximum limit that can be purchased, and the time limited of payment before extra charges are added to the bill. It is the crafter's responsibility to meet these terms and to pay on time. In fact, the reward for timely bill payment will be higher credit limits from your vendors.

So, even though you are a "self-employed" crafter, build a

relationship of integrity with your temporary or long-term "bosses" and you will build a sold business reputations and relationships that will aid your success in the crafting industry.

16

A Hobby Turns Into Successful Business

Bar S Monograms

"We serve over 500–600 high schools and 20 colleges with award and organization jackets; we've embroidered over 100,000 caps in the last year," Trella Suthers told me as I inquired about her home-based business, "Bar S Monograms" the company that custom-embroiders caps, jackets, golf shirts, and sports bags, for schools, small businesses and large corporations, and even monograms "cool down" horse blankets for use at racktracks. Customers range across the nation from California to Virginia, Alaska to Texas, from Mexico to South America. The more I heard, the more I felt that this thriving full-time business which began as a hobby was worth looking into.

Trella, a ranch wife from the western Oklahoma wide-open spaces 12 miles from the nearest town of Arnett, had helped her husband Mac for years in the showing and sales of registered Hereford cattle. In this sparsely populated area, their two children went to school, were active in Future Farmers of America, and showed the cattle they raised themselves. The whole family worked together in the Hereford business.

Then Trella became interested in embroidery and monogramming. When she first saw embroidery machines demonstrated at a fair in Dallas, this former home economics instructor had two ideas in mind: the machine could be a fun hobby and perhaps supplement their ranching income. "We had three children we wanted to support and two to send through the university. In order to do this, we need extra income," she says.

After spending three months researching machines, the cost, the market, and business possibilities, Trella talked her husband into trekking back to Dallas to purchase an embroidery machine. His reaction was a little less than enthusiastic, but after seeing what could be done on the machines, he became interested in investing in the machine and even in helping with the project. In the beginning, after finishing his ranch chores in the evening, Mac drew many of the first designs.

Shortly after the second visit to Dallas, a two-head embroidery machine was delivered to the Suthers' home. A company representative took three days teaching Trella the basics of operating the machine and left her with a thick manual to figure out the rest. Manual in hand, Trella and her neighbor tackled the operation. After a few days of study and trial and error, a beautiful finished product began to come off of the embroidery machine. Almost before Trella had complete mastery over the machine, the orders began to come in from FFA and Agriculture friends and associates who needed work done and had heard about her embroidery machine.

Today, Trella has no time to feed or show Hereford cattle. Husband Mac still does the cattle business as his main enterprise, although he does all the maintenance and mechanical work on their Monogram shop equipment, goes to trade shows with Trella and helps with exhibits. They needed more space, so the 40' by 80' metal building on their land in which they used to conduct cattle sales was converted to an embroidery shop. Today, Trella and her friend, Barbara, work full-time, along with ten employees Trella hired. She later purchased a twelve-head machine, with nine color, auto-color change and thread trimmers, and a one-head, four-head, and six-head machine. How did this business expand and grow? How did Suthers market her embroidery service?

Marketing Bar S Monograms

"Our first niche was the Ag (Agriculture) and FFA group," says Trella. Since she had taught Home Ec in the local high school, she had many friends in that and other schools. This created an immediate market in the high schools. Through the children, parents, and teachers Trella and Mac knew through FFA and 4-H, and associates in the agriculture business and college departments, they tapped into the markets in their own backyard.

The Suthers put their label on every piece that went out: "Screen printed/or embroidered by Bar S Monograms" with the phone number. Hundreds were purchased, each wearer making a walking advertisement. Some of the best advertising was word-of-mouth from satisfied customers.

"We try not to send anything out unless it is perfect," says Trella. From the time a cap comes in to the shop until it goes out in an order, it is handled by four people. Quality control is high. If there is anything wrong with one cap in an order of 100 caps, the order doesn't go out.

This excellent, top-notch quality is one of the secrets to success of Bar S Monograms. Whereas, some embroidery companies don't clip between letters, they employ one person to do just that—clip threads so the finished product will be the best. Using mostly women who are very particular and detail-oriented, (farm women who are diligent perfectionists, and do quality work) they have established a superior reputation. With that kind of attention to detail and quality, the word spreads quickly and the orders pour in.

The Next Success Secret: Dedication

To meet the demand of customers, Trella often is in her Monogram shop from early morning to late at night. "That's one of the secrets," she says, "You've got to love what you're doing, and be willing to work long hours."

"What has helped our business more than anything is *service,*" she adds. Bar S Monograms tries to keep their delivery to three weeks and do a lot of overtime to keep up—which is a major selling point.

"Do a lot of research *before* you start. And be willing to put your heart and soul into the business and look forward to long hours if you plan to make your business a success," Trella says.

DON'T GIVE UP!

There are fleeting moments when she wishes this still was a hobby and she had more free time. "When you work for someone else you can leave and go home. With your own business, you must be a dedicated self-starter." Growth always brings challenges, and from the opening of the Monogram shop in 1986, Bar-S has done nothing but grow. The business profits put both kids through college and their daughter through veterinary college.

Running a successful business also requires *determination*. Every business has its problems—whether it is the challenges of expansion and needing extra employees to keep up with the workload or keeping good records when you are so busy with production it's hard to eek out time.

> **"Nothing in the world can take the place of persistence. Talent will not; nothing is more common than unsuccessful men with talent. Genius will not; unrewarded genius is almost a proverb. Education will not; the world is full of educated derelicts. Persistence and determination alone are omnipotent."**
> —*Calvin Coolidge*

A person's greatness and success is not determined by his or her fame, position, or wealth but rather *what it takes to discourage that person*. What does it take to discourage you:

- things that don't go your way?
- expectations that are not met?
- someone that disapproves of how you did it?

Things that last usually require more time and determination than usual. An oak tree takes 60 years, while a mushroom only takes

6 hours of growth. Do you want your business to have the stability of an oak tree or a mushroom?[8]

From Brands To Monograms

When Trella first told people in the town about her idea for a monogram business, they laughed and said "There's no way you'll make it way out there in the country!" They asked how she went from brands to monograms.

She was willing to learn. Trella did have a background with fabrics and sewing, but that's a different skill than running a big embroidery machine. It takes at least six to eight months to become a good machine operator. Trella had only two and a half days of instruction on what the machine would do and had only a big manual to find out the rest on her own.

The monogram business is a high-tech business, with all the designs done on computer. "I had never been close to a computer, except through a store window, and had all that to learn. We produce all our own original designs on computer, and also have graphics arts computers for most of our lettering and logos for t-shirts." Going to seminars provided extra training, and hours spent pouring over manuals added up to more expertise on the machine. Now that the Suthers have the machines down pat, they focus on keeping up the business operations and hiring employees to run the machines.

Trella's biggest challenges are keeping up with deadlines, incredible amounts of book work, and government regulations, including taxes, unemployment insurance, etc. What helped her the most is having an accountant who advises her on workman's compansation, Social Security for employees, unemployment benefits. He figures her net profit every quarter and if suppliers' price increases have caused net profit to be down, advises her to raise her prices to keep up.

Tip: Hiring a good accountant can save you money, hassles, and legal problems. Although many home-based business people shy away from the expense of a professional accountant, and think

"I'll do it myself," actually a knowledgeable accountant is an important investment in your business. He or she can help you track expenses, set up a system of bookkeeping, alert you to tax deductions and changes in tax regulations affecting home and small businesses.

Overcoming Obstacles—Avoiding Pitfalls

"One of the hardest things I've dealt with in business has been employee relations," says Suthers. "Everyone I've hired I've known twenty years, and then I'm no longer friend but boss. It changes the whole picture; your relationship changes. That's been a challenge." Since she needed more employees to keep up with the work, dealing fairly with employees has been a challenge—and Bar S Monograms has ten full-time workers.

Employees must have withholding and Social Security taxes deducted.

Employers may be liable for federal unemployment taxes. If you are unsure whether your employees are independent contractors or truly your employees, contact the IRS and request Form #SS-8 plus any other printed information on employees' benefits or withholding taxes. (If a government agency determines that a person you have hired as contract labor is actually an employee, then you, as the employer, are responsible to pay all back taxes and penalties on such misclassifications.)

Another pitfall is recordkeeping. You have to keep accurate and complete records on every order because frequently a customer will call and say, "I'd like to get the same order I had made up two years ago—the same size lettering, the same thread colors, everything. So I keep and file each invoice indefinitely."

How to have orders picked up and delivered might appear a challenge in the sparsely populated western Oklahoma county where the Suthers live. "But UPS has been wonderful," says Trella. "They pick up and deliver right to our door and come every single day."

When the business continued to expand and expand Trella

was spending more and more nights working. It became hard to separate business from their own private life. This year she decided "I have to have a life," so she and her husband Mac took up golf. Now with their children out of college, on each evening and weekends, you can find the Suthers on the golf course. She works from 8:30 a.m. until 4:30 p.m., with thirty minutes for lunch. At 4:30 she heads for the nearby golf course instead of working a few more hours. "I have more confidence in my employees on the operating machines, and I'd rather pay them overtime than burn myself out."

Government regulations could be an obstacle, but Trella follows them to a "T." In the sewing business you can't hire anyone under sixteen; they can't even be on the floor of the sewing operations. Her accountant handles all of her labor reports and informs her of new regulations, unemployment benefits, workman's compensation, etc. "I've added health insurance benefits for all employees," she says.

Zoning is not a problem because, with their cattle cooperation in a rural area, they were already zoned commercial.

Networking—Finding Suppliers

In the beginning, finding suppliers was a major step. Networking with other people in the industry provided the way. The Suthers went to trade shows to find new products, to see what is being featured for the next season. They also attended seminars on networking, pricing, and marketing. Through these trade shows they met people to help find suppliers. (The Suthers still try to make two or three trade shows a year.) "I met a lady in Arkansas at a trade show, jotted down her telephone number, and when I looked for a supplier for materials, I called her. She'd been in the monogram and embroidery business for five years."

Go to trade shows, meet and network with people. If you have a problem, a home-based business associate may have faced and solved a similar problem and can help you figure it out.

To continue expanding their customer base, they set up six to eight exhibit booths a year at various conventions: the Athletic Coaches Convention, Agriculture conferences, the State FFA Convention, and even a local farm show.

Rural States See Home as Where the Jobs Are

Oklahoma is not the only state that is seeing the growth of home-based businesses in rural areas like Trella Suthers' Bar S Monograms, but it is one of the leaders in supporting them. "Rural states promote home businesses as a key to economic stability," said Barbara Marsh in *Enterprise*.[9] Economic-development officials in many states see home businesses as a steadying force for small towns and a way to retain jobs in rural communities.

Some states are starting networks of home businesses to offer marketing help, tax and other business tips, and networking opportunities. The following states have statewide home-based business associations: Colorado, Missouri, Nebraska, California, Pennsylvania, and South Dakota.

Marilyn Burns, a specialist on home-based business for the Oklahoma Extension Service, started one of the first statewide associations in America with about 500 home businesses in 1990. Ms. Burns and other experts present seminars on a wide range of topics (zoning, record-keeping, making a business plan, etc.), organize an annual state home business convention/trade show, organize local chapters, provide materials, and serve as a resource for people. Burns has also written a handbook for other states interested in setting up a similar service to promote and support home businesses, and addressed Governors at the White House on how to support home-based businesses in their state.

The Central Office for Home-Based Entrepreneurship, HES 135/Oklahoma State University, Stillwater, OK 74078, also publishes educational materials such as:

HOME-BASED BUSINESS: Legal Considerations
HOME-BASED BUSINESS: Putting It All Together
(Revised and Expanded)
Directory of Oklahoma Home-Based Business

To keep up with the latest trends, fashions, helpful hints for problem areas, and the latest information concerning new products and equipment, here are the important Trade Journals for the embroidery/monogram business:

> *Impressions Magazine*
> P. O. Box 41529
> Nashville, TN 37204
> (800) 207-1154
> (Contains lots of articles pertaining to embroidery,
> screen printing, and monogramming business)

> *Embroidery Business News*
> P. O. Box 5400
> Scottsdale, AZ 85261-5400
> 602) 990-1101

> *Stitches* Magazine
> P. O. Box 12960
> Overland Park, KS 66282-2960
> (913) 341-1300

For more information on Bar S Monograms write:

> Bar S Monograms, Inc.,
> Trella Suthers,
> Rt. 2, Box 86,
> Arnett, OK 73832,
> (405) 885-7783.

17

From Fast-Track Ad World to Home Studio

Greeting Card Business: Drawing Her Way Back Home

Debi Hamuka-Falkenham sits with her children around the dining table with textbooks, pencils, magic markers, and science projects spread out before them. It's Monday morning, and homeschooling is in full swing. But it wasn't always that way for Debi, a commercial artist who once kept pace with the fast-track life of the advertising world.

After attending Paier School of Art in Hamden, Connecticut, and taking a cartooning course at the Museum of Cartoon Art in New York City, Debi Hamuka-Falkenham did advertising and cartooning work on a contract basis for ITT, General Electric, and other corporations for fourteen years. But her priorities shifted to greeting cards and designing other gift products because she was mothering three children and finding the fast-track advertising world a poor companion with family life.

"The advertising work had severe deadlines and high pressure," Debi said. In fact, experts say that advertising agency work rates up there with the highest stress occupations. "The greeting card industry is more relaxed, and fits better with my family responsibilities in this season of mothering."

Much of Debi's greeting card work is contracted with established greeting card companies. For example, she has a line of children's Valentine cards commissioned by Dayspring. For Contemporary

Designs, she creates a line of cards for parents to send to their children in college.

Landing Commission Assignments

Many of Debi's commissioned assignments come as a result of displaying her work in greeting card trade shows. She recommends especially *Surtex: Designs for Every Surface,* a trade show run in conjunction with the New York Stationery Show each May, and the New York Licensing Show in June. She also recommends establishing contacts through the Greeting Card Creative Network.

Greeting Card Associations, Networks, Guilds

Greeting Card Creative Network—Organization for artists doing commissioned work for established greeting card companies. Free information packet. Membership benefits include newsletter, workshops, annual talent directory.

Greeting Card Association—Association for greeting card publishers who want to reach the wholesale and retail markets. Free info packet: 1350 New York Avenue, NW, Suite 615 Washington, DC 20005 (202) 393-1780, FAX (202) 393-0336

Graphic Artists Guild, Cartoonist Guild 11 West 20th Street, 8th Floor New York, NY 11011-3704 (212) 463-7730, FAX (212) 463-8779 Free Information packet available.

Greeting Card Resources

This Business of Art (Cochrane) is a guide to business practices for artists, including contracts, copyrights, the artist as seller and exhibitor, royalties, etc.

Publishing Your Art as Cards and Posters, Harold Davis, 1990. The Consultant Press, 163 Amsterdam Avenue #201, New York, NY 10023

The Complete Guide to Greeting Card Design and Illustration, Eva Szebo, North Light Books, 1507 Dana Avenue, Cincinnati, OH 45207

Greetings Magazine, Mackay Publishing, 309 Fifth Avenue, New York, NY 10016 (Contains useful trade information for the retail greeting card and gift market)

"Most artists are very helpful," says Debi. "We network about companies and exchange experiences and views on how fair each one is. It's a casual network, but a valuable one. If a company wants to work with me and I'm not sure about the organization and their policies, I can call other artists that I've met doing trade shows to check on issues such as: Are they offering a fair price, a fair deal on the royalty and advance or flat fee?" Perhaps the artist knows someone who received a better advance or working agreement, and they can give Debi information which helps her negotiate a favorable contract.

If she is negotiating or is offered a commission or deal with a company on the phone she buys time by responding, "Let me call my Business Manager" (her husband). Not making a hasty decision on the phone also gives time to network with an artist-friend who can advise her.

Copyrighting Your Greeting Card Designs

A copyright is government protection which prevents your greeting card designs, (book, newsletter, sculpture, photographs, presentation, video or report from being reproduced and marketed in a similar form by someone else. You can register for a copyright with the U.S. Copyright Office. For a work in the visual arts, you need Form VA. It takes six to eight weeks or more to process your application. Ask for free brochures and pamphlets such as *Making It Legal* which gives you information on copyrighting, trademarks, and patents. Write to:

Publications Section, LM-455
U. S. Copyright Office
Library of Congress
Washington, D. C. 20559

You can also order application forms and information by calling the "Forms and Circulars Hot-line" at (202) 287-9100.

Network with others! Meet and exchange phone numbers and ideas through industry trade shows and other art events. Women in the greeting card industry really help each other. "One artist in particular gave me a lot of encouragement and support when I was just getting started," says Debi. There is a great sense of camaradie among established greeting card artists.

Best Tip for Greeting Card Homeworkers

- Don't be afraid to ask for help

- Put pride in your back pocket and be teachable

- Remember, there is much to learn from others who have trod the path you are on!

- Join business or professional organizations to network with others in your field. Also join local and state home business associations.

- Subscribe to newsletters and trade journals in your industry to get the names of people you can network with and to find the suppliers and information you need

- Always be willing to *give*, not just to receive help. Be open to opportunities to encourage and give leads and help to those in your circle or network of friends in the industry.

- Stay in touch with a friend who is in your field or in a different one; have coffee together, talk about your triumphs and struggles, receive her encouragement. It is good to get out of your studio or office once in a while!

Trade Shows for Greeting Card Artists

Surtex and the New York Stationery Show
George Little Management, Inc.
2 Park Avenue, Suite 1100
New York, NY 10016-6598
(800) 292-4560, FAX(212) 685-6598

New York Licensing Show
Expocon Management Associates
7 Cambridge Drive
P. O. Box 1019
Trumbull, CT 06611
(203) 374-1411, ext. 106, FAX(203) 374-9667

Creating a Personal Line of Greeting Cards and Products

In addition to commissioned projects, Debi works on her own greeting cards and related products. She has designed a greeting card and t-shirt line for people on a diet. In addition, her love of kids inspired an alphabet t-shirt line for children, and a fabric line for pediatric hospitals. She also sells her own greeting cards at various shows.

Self-Publishing Greeting Cards

- *Develop a professional-looking catalog.*
- Before investing in an expensive print run of greeting cards, practice designs, take art courses, and read everything you can about creating graphics and running a business. Subscribe to a trade journal in the greeting card field.
- *Think:* What will make a customer want to buy and send this card? Visit card shops and do your own market research
- *Start small.* The secret to success for one self-published greeting card artist, Amy Webster—"Blessed are These" line was to start small and grow slowly. "You can hand-color your first designs and try to sell them at gift shops to learn what you need to know," Amy says.
- *Never forget you are providing a me-to-you message.* You have to be in touch with yourself and with other people and their needs to communicate effectively through greeting cards,
- *Find your niche.* Debi found her niche in children's products, individualized lines of cards for dieters; Amy found hers with elegantly designed cards with an old-fashioned look which appeal to women who with traditional values who are family-centered. Another artist found his niche in sports cards—Charlie Trainer designed four-color photograph cards of various sports (now in ski shops throughout the Northwest). Always be looking for your special niche.

Finding Your Greeting Card Market

Possible markets for your self-published greeting card line include:

- Grocery stores
- Gift shops
- Beauty salons
- Hospital gift shops
- Postal service outlets
- Florists
- Direct market to organizations (Weight Watchers, or Compassionate Friends),lawyers, doctors and medical associations, schools and colleges
- Bookstores

Pricing Your Cards

- While you do your market research at stores that sell greeting cards, check *pricing*.
- Try a formula: Materials and overhead costs + labor - number of units = selling price/unit
- Check with other greeting card artists
- Refer to *Greetings* Magazine, *Artist's Market* annual, and publications in the industry

The Family Room: Balancing Time and Priorities

"It is possible to work at home with children and retain the right to be their primary caregiver," says Lindsey O'Conner, mother of four and author of *Working at Home*.[10] How do you really run a business with children, especially little ones around? "Some people will tell you it cannot be done successfully, at least with any degree of professionalism. Others may tell you it's a breeze. . . You just have to be creative and have a lot of patience, endless energy, and a good supply of crayons!"

How did Debi find time to design new products and run her home business with three small children to care for? At first, she had a babysitter come in a few hours a day to help with the children.

On days when she had no help, she worked early in the morning, during nap time, or at night.

Debi keeps a copy of Proverbs 3:5-6 nearby as she works in her studio as a guide for keeping her business in perspective. She also appreciates her children as a major source of inspiration and creativity for her work.

Still, when her freelancing for companies and own creative products became more and more successful, she found herself torn between family and deadlines, work and kids. "I became almost a workalcoholic," Debi said. "It's easy to burn yourself out and both you and your family suffers."

Debi is trying a more relaxed approach instead of trying to do every project *this month or this year.* "Society says you need instantaneous success. I was so geared in a career world, that I'd put my worth on my success," she adds.

"But who's going to hug me when the day is through—my children or my career? I have the rest of my life for my career; my kids are only going to be little a short time."

Debi now is homeschooling her children in conjunction with her greeting card art business, and she finds it a great opportunity to have separate, concentrated times with them.

Making Home Business Work With Kids

- Hire baby sitters, mother's helper, or trade care with a friend daily or a few times a week to have specific blocks of time to work.

- Be flexible. Try working during naps, in the evenings (with spouse handy for wake-ups or bedtime rituals), or early in the morning. Adjust your work schedule to your children's schedules as they grow.

Tips on Working at Home

- Have an office space that is separate from the main flow of the house for the blocks of time you do manage to carve out for work.

- Plan blocks for heavy-duty thinking, designing products, or composing written reports when your children are napping or happily occupied with your spouse.

- Keep a positive outlook and remember why you wanted to work near your kids in the first place!

- Plan times for focused attention for you and your child: to listen to her stories and dreams, to play at the park together, read a favorite book aloud, to just be together without the demands of the business phone ringing.

- If you have work to do that doesn't demand your undivided attention, you could set up a little play "office area" near you with an old invoice pad, pencil, old typewriter (look at garage sales), and old (real) telephone for your child to use during certain times.

- Equipment like a cordless phone, separate personal and business lines, an answering machine, making working at home with kids less stressful and more efficient.

- Know your limits and don't try to accomplish everything *today*. Avoid trying to do too much, and you'll help avoid burnout and a crabby disposition.

- Get your older children to help by: playing with younger child, helping you with a mailing, stuffing envelopes, filling orders, etc. Some homeworkers pay their children and put part of the payment for services in a savings account for their college funds (good tax deduction). Older children can learn how to answer the phone, how to wait for a few minutes if an important call is in process, and be a good role model for the younger kids.

Wisdom On Working At Home With Children
Set ground rules.

It is important to establish a set of rules and guidelines that will work for you and your family. Make it clear to your children what you expect, what is allowed, and what is not allowed when you are working.

Include your children in your work when you can.

It makes them feel more a part of your life. At the same time your children can learn what it is that you do, gain specific skills, responsibility, and the value of hard work.

Schedule breaks with your children.

Implement a "kids' time," in which you plan a special activity or outing, and let them know when you will be finished working.[11]

When working at home you can watch your children grow, be there for an after-school chat, for first steps, first words, and school plays. The benefits are endless. It's not easy every day, but it's worth it! With flexibility, creative planning, a supportive spouse who is willing to pitch in, good equipment, and a "big picture" view of priorities—that there is a season for everything, and that *everything doesn't have to be accomplished in this month or year*—you can make it work.

Study the Card Counters

One of the best ways to do market research for the greeting card industry is to head for the stores that sell cards and spend unrushed time studying the product lines.

Take notes on what kind of cards each company carries, the tones of various cards, the artistic styles of various companies, punctuation styles (Hallmark, for instance, uses a lot of exclamation marks)

There are four basic categories of cards: Sentimental/conventional; Humorous; and Studio/contemporary; Personal expression. What category would your cards fit in?

More Resources for Greeting Cards

Writer's Market
Cincinnati, Ohio: Wrier's Digest Books, one for each current year. Usually available in most bookstores and libraries, and includes a list of greeting-card companies; then you can send for their writer's guidelines and company's current needs.

Artist's and Writer's *Market List*
National Association of Greeting Card Publishers,
600 Pennsylvania Avenue, Suite 300, Washington, D.C 20003
(Send an SASE and ask for the *Artist's and Writer's Market List*)

18

Helping Others Heal

Lifeskills, Inc.

One of the most interesting and exciting things about many of the home-based entrepreneurs I interviewed in the past few years is how a business evolves when you are following your heart and passion, using your talents, and are attentive to the needs of the people or market you serve. Many homeworkers find that although they start in one direction or focus, as they learn and the business grows, it may lead them in another direction—perhaps a related one, but not one that was planned from the beginning. That's part of the beauty and adventure of home-based pursuits.

Valerie Acuff's experience is a good example of how a business or service evolves. For eight years she was a director of a major insurance company, running 28 sales offices in California and managing a national financial planning division for her company. She also designed training for sales and management.

However, when the company sold in 1990, the entire firm was restructured and Valerie's position was eliminated, not an uncommon turn of events in corporate takeovers. Not a person to sit around and feel sorry for herself, Valerie immediately planned a career to help women who, like herself, who had been laid off.

> **In every adversity there are the seeds of an
> equal or greater opportunity.**
> —*Clement Stone*

Career consulting gave Valerie the opportunity to see the many women who couldn't go full speed ahead on a new career, be at peace with themselves, or have a good relationship with God until they cleared their issues and relationships with the men in their lives. Seeing this need, she started a Tuesday night support group on relationships called "Lifeskills for Women" using Henry Cloud's book *Changes That Heal.* People began to ask for private counseling and for her to conduct workshops on setting boundaries. Churches approached her about presenting at marriage retreats and women's workshops. So "Lifeskills" began to grow, eventually eliminating the career counseling part of the business.

"As the Lifeskills groups and retreats took off, it showed us what we were all about," Valerie says.

Before career counseling is totally phased out, take Valerie's "Entrepreneur Appraisal" on page 191.

Being weak in an area does not mean you should throw away the idea of starting your business. Having a low score in the financial areas of the appraisal, for example, shows that you will need help and advice from a professional accountant to set up your bookkeeping system, help you be accountable, and keep you on track financially. If you are easily distracted from the task at hand, and your day usually has a chaotic feel to it, you need to get some help on time-management and basic planning of your day with certain hours for office work, time for family, recreation, errands, etc.

Valerie's husband, Walt, a licensed psychotherapist, eventually began conducting "Lifeskills for Men" groups when repeatedly asked for a weekly program like the one Valerie leads for women. They joined forces as the focus shifted from career counseling to full-time counseling, retreats, and workshops, helping people learn skills for more effective marriages, happier families, and happier, more successful careers or ministries. They also run a domestic violence program called "Learning to Live, Learning to Love."

The Acuffs sectioned 2,000 square feet of their Colorado Springs, Colorado home for a library, office, storage area, bathroom, counseling office, a large conference room that comfortably holds 40, and three work stations.

Entrepreneur Appraisal

Assess your personal potential to operate a home-based business. Circle a number for each statement to indicate how well it describes you or your feelings.

1 = not at all, 2 = sometimes, 3 = often, 4 = usually, 5 = always

1	2	3	4	5	I like to be in charge, and usually lead groups in which I work.
1	2	3	4	5	I tend to see the "whole picture" and all aspects of any project.
1	2	3	4	5	I am a leader of people. Others look to me for direction.
1	2	3	4	5	I realistically assess my talents and abilities.
1	2	3	4	5	I ask for advice from experts when I need help.
1	2	3	4	5	I am thorough and accurately complete tasks I begin.
1	2	3	4	5	I enjoy solving problems and view obstacles as opportunities.
1	2	3	4	5	I schedule my day and activities and stick to it.
1	2	3	4	5	Risk-taking gives me a feeling of excitement.
1	2	3	4	5	I delegate work to others and remove myself from the project, accepting others' processes and results.
1	2	3	4	5	I usually bounce back very quickly after a setback.
1	2	3	4	5	I am willing to devote myself to my business.
1	2	3	4	5	My attention is not easily diverted from tasks.
1	2	3	4	5	I have a planned budget that I do not exceed.
1	2	3	4	5	I don't usually buy from door-to-door or telephone solicitors.
1	2	3	4	5	I accept responsibility for the outcome of projects I undertake.
1	2	3	4	5	Disappointments and delays do not deter me from plans or goals I have set for myself.
1	2	3	4	5	I am goal-oriented and have a one-year, five-year, and 10-year plan.
1	2	3	4	5	I balance my checkbook every month.

Entrepreneur Appraisal Scoring—Add the circled numbers. If you scored 80 or above, you should have no problem operating a home-based business. If you scored below 60, you may want to look at those items in which you scored lowest and ask yourself, "What prevents me from doing those things?"

(Entrepreneur Appraisal used by permission of Lifeskills, Inc., Valerie Acuff)

Working Successfully As A Husband-Wife Team

When husband and wife work together in a home enterprise, there is great potential for cooperation and balancing each other's strengths and weaknesses. There is also great possibility of tension and stress on the relationship, depending on *how* you work together. According to Valerie, some advance discussion and planning can make a big difference.

"For a woman, it is important to know what her gifts are and to be confident in them," she says. "It's so easy for women to be intimidated by their husbands in a partnership situation. But by being aware and acknowledging your gifts, you'll develop the freedom to share them and *know what your part is* and also know what your spouse's part is in the business."

In the Acuffs' situation, Walt is a licensed therapist, whereas Valerie is a non-licensed, registered psychotherapist. But Valerie has the gifts to do the major part of the retreats they offer. She does people-processing, facilitates materials and essentials, and coordinates everything for the weekend or week-long event. Walt assists her in whatever needs to be done. It's what she does best, for as Valerie says, "It's not about psychology but about helping people to get unstuck and get on with their career or ministry."

Valerie is more introverted than her husband and operates more from her head than her heart. She is more tightly structured, than Walt, who 'goes with the flow.' He is also very relational, extroverted and more feeling-oriented than she. They are a good balance for each other, which enhances their partnership.

The Acuffs developed a mission statement for their marriage early. When a problem arises, they refer to the mission statement and eliminate whatever is interfering with it. "Our purpose is to do our service together without egos in the way, so one of us backs off if we are jeopardizing the relationship or mission," she said.

Walt and Valerie advise couples develop their own mission statement. "Just like a corporation has such a written statement of purpose that keeps them on target, couples need to stay on target.

We use ours to determine our course of action when making plans or when opportunities are presented to us."

Their working relationship is also assisted by holding business meetings every six to eight weeks. They may bring in an objective person, one of the Lifeskills board members or someone who has observed their working together and is an expert in a certain area. At the business meeting they identify: concerns; what is being overlooked; and how they can fill in the gaps. The critical agenda at the meeting is *how are we doing in our goals in a specific area?*

Setting Boundaries

Valerie sees the biggest pitfall for home-business men and women is *boundaries,* and especially the *lack of boundaries* between their home/personal life and their work/business (related to time management, space, phone, and other demands of the business).

Setting a boundary between when and where you are at work or at home is important, she says. "If your office is in the kitchen, it's the kiss of death," she says. "People are in and out; it's hard to turn your back on interruptions."

First advice on boundaries: if you cannot have a separate office, parition one using a folding screen.

Next, write a daily schedule and attempt to follow it. "I have a daily schedule of being in the office from 9:00 a.m. to 3:00 p.m. From 3 p.m. to 5 p.m., I'm in my house, and from 5:00 p.m. to 9:00 p.m. I'm in the office again, three days a week and Saturday morning."

Valerie plans an afternoon to do all her errands at one time. She exercises with a video at home during out-of-office time. And once or twice a week she and Walt rent a movie to watch in the evening just to relax. Counseling can be so draining.

Schedule fun time together and do not discuss business during that time. (If you work together daily, it's hard not to discuss it, but make a "no business talk" pact.) "Every Friday night is our date night. We go to a movie, go out to dinner alone, or curl up with popcorn and a video. And we don't talk about the counseling or retreat coming up," she adds.

Because they work many weekends on retreats and speaking, they block out one weekend a month to *not work*. They may go hiking, stay home and take the phones off the hook, or take a short trip. These weekends off are important to avoid physical and emotional exhaustion.

A big year-long planner with grease pencil hung on the wall helps tremendously. The Acuffs mark their birthdays and those of their four grown children. They record scheduled workshops, seminars, and longer retreats, including travel. At least once a year they go to England and Scotland to conduct training retreats and some group work.

Set some boundaries for business and home telephone, so calls won't drive you crazy. People pleasers have the hardest time setting boundaries between home and office because they always want to be available and hate to disappoint or displease the callers by not answering (even if there is an answering machine). People pleasers may have to put a sign over the phone listing the hours they answer the office phone. An "Office is Closed" sign on the door should also state office hours.

Separate home and office phone lines help set boundaries, but make sure that you cannot hear the office phone ring all over the house except during office hours. "We've got four phone lines that ring in the office: a fax line, office line, home line, and another line," says Valerie. "We don't answer the office lines when it's at-home time. It rings only in the office area."

Promoting Lifeskills

In December 1994, Valerie and Walt began their *Lifeskills* newsletter to spread the word about their counseling services, retreats, and small groups. "The results were wonderful," she says. They include a personal message, a human interest story and testimonials from people who have attended their retreats and programs.

"I believe people are more interested in how our programs helped one single person, than they are in numbers and general results," she adds.

For more information on Lifeskills, Inc. call (719) 594-9936.

19

From Layoff To Creative Business

Smallfolk Dolls

In January 1992, when Evelyn Lopes of Middletown, Connecticut, was laid off from her job at Aetna Life and Casualty Company after eight years, she pondered where to go with her life. The former computer programmer didn't want to take unemployment compensation. She needed income, but she didn't want to go back to the corporate world. During her severance pay period, Evelyn prayed and asked God for guidance on how to make a living. But she didn't stop there. She began to think about creative ways to generate income and purposed to be alert to everything around her.

Two weeks after her prayer she saw woman on television making Easter bunnies with heavy gauge textured paper and thought, "I could do that." However, she had a new slant on the craft of dollmaking. She remembered from her childhood the lack of black culture in books, toys, and dolls. As a little girl, she wondered why there were no black dolls, especially a realistic depiction of the variety of physical features and colors of the black culture.

It is the greatest of all mistakes to do nothing, because you can only do little. Do what you can.
—*Sydney Smith*

When Evelyn went to a fabric store to buy the textured paper in all different colors, the idea emerged to make an African doll. After research at the library and several more trips to the piece-goods shop, her first African doll dressed in red, white, green, and black, was created. Named "Cleo," her first folk-art doll was made of heavy twisted paper for the body and crepe wool for hair. She sent it as a gift to her good friend Penny, who had a black doll collection. Soon she was twisting and sculpting the textured paper to create a multicultural, paper community of Smallfolk representing people of Africa, Spain, East India, and America.

Evelyn desired to foster a sense of history, identity and self-esteem in black children. Her *Smallfolk* dolls portray black people in all their diversity. And the market's response to the dolls proves she met her goals. Although her dolls do not have facial features, each has its own unique personality, from the historical figures like Frederick Douglass to the Christmas figures of Mary and Joseph, the Three Wise Men and angels. One family of her dolls was based on her relatives and other people she knew while growing up, complete with humorous touches. Each doll is defined by its style of dress, hair color and texture, and skin.

Evelyn began by giving her Smallfolk dolls away, and after a month or more she recalled asking God for a way to make a living and *this was it!* "I was giving them away, and everybody went crazy," Lopes said. "They said, 'Evelyn, you can sell these.'" Suddenly, her home business was born. The first Smallfolk dolls for sale were ready in April 1992. They were distributed mainly by family and friends, through word-of-mouth, a mailing of holiday catalogs, and networking during a family vacation in Puerto Rico.

Spreading the Word Through Community Service

One way Evelyn spread the word about her Smallfolk business was to become involved with community fund-raisers. She purposefully contributed her dolls to the community. She donated her African Collection to the Lincoln-Basset Elementary School in New Haven, Connecticut, for display. She visited nursery schools to share her dolls with children. She also conducted workshops to show the New Haven students how to make paper-sculpted dolls.

Lopes donated time to teach members of her Middletown church how to make Smallfolk carolers to sell at the annual holiday fair. She taught adult craft classes in paper dollmaking and donated her dolls to benefit the high school and other community bazaars and charities.

Because of Evelyn's community efforts and the resulting exposure, Smallfolk Paper Art was featured in newspaper and magazine articles across the state opening a wider market. The free exposure from articles even led to television programs featuring her dolls. Her first big break came when the owner of a boutique in New Haven, Conneticut, displayed her African Collection. Her historical figures also caught the eye of a businessman who took them to the Black Expo in Atlanta, which produced more orders.

Word-of-mouth led a Dallas shop owner to begin taking orders, sight unseen, from customers all over the country. Without ever buying any advertising, her home business took off and generated orders from Los Angeles to Iowa, Texas to Washington, D.C. She became so busy that her teenage son and husband pitched in to help. Her husband, Matthew, also designed and helped produce a Smallfolk Christmas catalog.

Discouragement-Busters When Your Job Is Lost

There's no doubt about it—sometimes a closed door can open an exciting new window of opportunity and direction. *Here are Evelyn's tips on handling a lay-off productively and maybe even developing your own business in the process:*

- Follow a regular routine. If you find yourself without a job, get up at the regular time, shower and shave, eat regularly, exercise, and go to bed at the same time. "Maintaining a routine is very important, because when your life is disrupted by job loss, you find yourself disoriented," says Lopes. "I felt a little low at first after being laid off, rested for two weeks and then decided to use the time to gather information instead of lying in bed and sulking."

- Get centered. Get quiet, and admit that you're afraid, instead of denying or stuffing your feelings. Get past your feelings by talking to your family about your situation and seeking support from friends and associates. The anxiety won't go away in a day, but if you begin to think about what you really want to do, do some research and look around your town, you will move in a positive direction.

- Look for a product or service people are driving miles to get: Can you perform that service? What can you do to make the product or service better so people will buy it from you? Find out what people want or need to find your own niche.

- Pay attention. If you seek a product or service to fill, pay attention when you think you have found it. "It's almost like when you were a child and played the 'hot and cold' game," says Lopes. "Remember when you'd get close to the prize, the exhilaration of getting 'warm?' When you know it's what you're supposed to do, when you find it, the momentum builds. It's like someone saying: 'You're hot!'"

- Do plenty of research on the service or product you want to provide. Go to a library where there are books, magazines and other free resources. Do research *at the library*. It gets you out so you are not working in a vacuum.

- Design some business cards on your computer or go to a local print shop and order some. Even if you don't have a business name yet, have a business card with your name, address, phone and fax number, and take them wherever you go. When you attend business seminars and entrepreneur meetings, give out your card. Talk to people about what you'd like to do and they will remember you if you give them a card.

Developing an Effective Business Card

Your business card is relatively inexpensive and a small part of your overall budget. But, it is one of the most important tools in your home business advertising. It's your passport or introduction to the business world. The business card shows you are a professional, reflects your personality, and projects the concept or image of your business.

- Go to your local printers and look through their portfolio of business cards. Study business cards in your field (also look at the ones you've collected in your drawer or roll-a-dex) and take notice of different types and styles.

Creating an Effective Business Card

- A business card should be clear, simple, and include your: name, business name, address or post office box, phone number, "by appointment only" (if applicable), and logo or line of copy to explain what you're about. If you have an artistic friend who could help you design a logo, that's fortunate; or you could use the clip art or graphics available on most word processing and desk-top publishing software. *Make sure your logo relates directly to the company identity you're trying to establish.* Your theme should be expressed through the combination of words and graphics.

- When you look at samples, consider: why do some stand out? What colors and type styles strike you as effective? Which copy or slogans are catchy?

- Draw a sketch to scale in order to determine your card layout and help you visualize it.

- When you have a good mock-up, discuss prices with your printer. Remember that once the ink is in place, you may receive a discount by having a larger quantity printed at one time.

- If you don't have business stationery yet, consider tying it in with your business card for an overall impression. If printed at the same time as your cards, you may save money.

- Be original but avoid being too cutesy or garish with your business card. Think about your target market and what impression you are trying to reflect.

- Avoid cluttering your card with too much print. You may discourage people from reading your card to learn about your business and where to find your product or service. Aim for a good balance between negative and positive space (i.e., white space and copy).

Networking and Staying Abreast In Your Field

Attend Small Business Administration meetings. Call your local SBA office and get your name on the mailing list. Attend their seminars on how to start a small or home-based business, how to write a business plan, how to keep good records, etc. The SBA is a great source of information.

How to Contact the Small Business Administration (SBA)

For information on services the SBA offers the home and small business, call 1-800-827-5722.

SBA On-Line/General Access Call: 1-800-697-4636. SBA On-Line/Downloading Files and Mailbox Access: 1-900-463-4636.

To locate the Small Business Development Center nearest you for seminars, resources, and information, call 1-800-8-ASK-SBA.

- Network with people who attend SBA meetings and seminars because the people there are probably ahead of you and can give you suggestions and help you find good information. (Home and small business people tend to help each other.)

- Buy trade magazines in the area of your focus and interests. See what trends are current and what is happening in that industry. What was the big item last year?

- If you are a crafter, join a craft guild, go to the shows, and see what is out there. Ask what people are buying? Can you improve it?

- Go to your local Chamber of Commerce, another good source of information on all kinds of businesses. For instance, when Lopes needed to know where and when the craft shows take place in order to display her dolls, the Chamber of Commerce sent her a brochure and calendar of all the year's craft shows throughout the state.

When You Find Your 'Niche': First Steps

- Once you have established your business, *name it.* Then call the State Department of Revenue Service or state Tax Commission to get a sales and use tax permit. With a tax number, you can buy supplies and equipment tax-free, wholesale, or at a discount.

- Then go to City Hall and *register* your business name and they will give you a Certificate of Adoption of Trade Name. This registers your business with the city, so if anyone wants your product or services, you are a legitimate business.

- Once your business is up and going, you may want to *design a new business card* that accurately describes your business or service. Keep the cards with you at all times and hand them out. You never know where your business card will lead. That person might not need your product, but may pass it along.

- To get name recognition, *volunteer your product or service* to your community. Display your products at the library and have a sign with your business name so people recognize it and attach it to your work.

- *Call the local newspaper* and tell them your story. Perhaps they will feature an article about you and your business, which is excellent free advertising.

"When one door closes, another one opens—especially if you're looking for the new door," says Evelyn. "Look at lay-off as an adventure, an opportunity. My being laid off by a corporation opened up a whole new world to me."

Six Ways to Spread the Word With Your Business Card

1. *Tell neighbors, friends and relatives* about your business and help them spread the news by giving two or three of your business cards to each friend: one to keep and two to give away.

2. *Tack your business card on community bulletin boards.*

3. *Enclose your card in business letters and correspondence.*

4. *When you do a demonstration or seminar, pass out your business cards to the audience,* or put a supply of them on your display table for prospective customers to take.

5. *Always have a stack of your cards available on display tables* and exhibit booths when you are presenting *your products or service.*

5. *Enlarge your business card and create an oversized one that* could be used as a bookmark or something useful (an art shop made a ruler on one side, their information on the other).

New Directions for Smallfolk

In late 1994, Smallfolk evolved from sculptured paper dolls to soft dolls, but kept the multicultural theme. "I want to create and produce dolls that children can play with," says Evelyn. The paper ones are collectors' dolls for adults, and not for touching. She felt there was a niche for multicultural soft dolls, so in December, 1994 Evelyn discontinued the production of paper dolls and began working on a prototype for a soft doll.

By calling around and networking, Lopes was directed by the Entrepreneurial Support Center run by the Small Business Administration to a manufacturer in Hong Kong that could make a mock-up of the doll she had designed for a good price. Then she had individual women crafters in Connecticut make up copies of the mock-up doll.

Prototypes were necessary because she was trying to get her dolls into the mass retail market. "I don't want the dolls to be expensive, and that is why I'm choosing this market, so everyone can afford one." She contacted discount stores such as K-Mart corporate offices, Toys R Us, and retail stores, to make connections and send the new soft dolls to buyers. She also researched Freight forwarders to determine prices to ship dolls from Hong Kong to the United States.

"You are always learning new things in a home business. Life is never boring!" says Lopes. "People come to you because you've accomplished something, and you're not stuck in a routine 9 to 5 job." Evelyn has no desire to return to the corporate world, and is elated with the adventure of home business and new direction with the soft multicultural dolls. "I thank God now for my lay-off! I'd never have left there on my own because of the money and what I thought was 'security.'"

Practical, Inexpensive Ways To
Promote Your Home Business

Like Evelyn, get involved in community projects, which not only give you a chance to "give back" and help others draw attention to your business. A floral shop owner volunteered to decorate a museum in their city for the holiday. They received a lot of free publicity for their efforts.

When a news article is written about you in the newspaper or a magazine, share it by having it reprinted as a promotional flyer. Tape it to a standard sheet of typing paper, type information about your service, and run off a quantity of the promotional sheet. Add it to your customer's packages, your outgoing correspondence, etc.

Create a promotional flyer on bright paper that describes your products or service. You could include tips that would help your customers or appeal to the market you want to reach. Include the flyer in customer packages and mailings. Give it to interested friends and family members, and tack it to community and church bulletin boards.

Once you have a core of regular customers or a mailing list, publish your own simple newsletter, catalog, or regular bulletin to inform people of new products and to promote your business.

For more information on Smallfolk write:

Smallfolk Paper Art
5211 Town Place
Middletown, CT 06457

Resources for Dollmaking

The Serious Dollmaker
Mimi's Books and Supplies
P. O. Box 662-SD1
Point Pleasant,NJ 08742

Dollmaking:
Projects and Plans and The Teddy Bear Review
P. O. Box 1948
Marion, OH 43305
(800) 347-6969

Doll Crafter
30595 Eight Mile
Livonia, MI 48152-1798

Teddy Bear and Friends
900 Frederick Street
Cumberland, MD 21502

Appendix A

National, State, and Local Organizations and Centers Offering Home-Based Business Support

1. **Small Business Development Centers:** Located throughout the U.S., SBDC's are usually affiliated with colleges and universities. The SBDC offers free individual counseling with experienced consultants on staff to work with homebusinesses on solving problems in your business, bookkeeping issues, taxes, developing and marketing products. Most SBDC services are at no or minimal charge. They also sponsor inexpensive business seminars and offer publications. Call Small Business Answer Desk at (800) 8 ASK-SBA for the Small Business Development Center in your area.

2. **Cooperative Extension Services:** Every state has Cooperative Extension Service Centers, also called Agricultural Extension Service. They have free resources for home and small businesses, eduction opportunities and seminars, consulting help such as connecting you with the right person to make a prototype of a product you hope to manufacture and market. Contact the County Extension Office for the location nearest you.

3. **Vocational Technical Education (Vo-Tech)** Centers and locations in each state offer business management assistance for start-up, small and home-based business owners.

4. **Small Business Administration** or **SBA**
   490 3rd St., S.W.
   Washington, DC 20416 (202) 205-7777

The SBA "Answer Desk": For general inquiries about services the SBA offers (800) 827-5722
For SBA Publications (booklets and videotapes) call (202) 205-6665 or write:
P. O. Box 30
Denver, CO 80201-0030

5. **SBA Government Contracting Division** offers free information on government buying methods, specifications and size criteria, bidding methods and more. A Government Contracting Specialist is on staff to assist you in obtaining government and Defense Department contracts. Call 1-800-8 ASK-SBA for the SBA Government Contracting Division nearest you.

6. **SCORE, Service Corps. of Retired Executives:** Part of the SBA, SCORE's experts are experienced executives from a wealth of industries who give advice on everything from pricing your services and marketing your products to setting up bookkeeping systems. For the local office of SCORE near you, call (800) 634-0245.

7. **Internal Revenue Service:** For free publications pertinent to home businesses such as "Guide to Free Tax Services," "Recordkeeping for a Small Business," IRS pub. 583, "Tax Guide for Small Business," IRS Pub. 334, and "Business Use of Your Home," IRS Pub. 587, call (800) 829-3676. Call (800) 829-1040 to speak with the taxpayer education coordinator. The IRS Education Department offers workshops, seminars, and business tax-kit counseling.

8. **U.S. Department of Commerce,** Office of Consumer Affairs, Washington, DC 20233, and your State Department of Commerce offer guides for small businesses and free booklets such as "Advertising, Packaging and Labelling" and information regarding product warranties, product safety. The Office of Consumer Affairs also offers advice and technical assistance to businesses on problems of concern to consumers.

9. **U.S. Department of Labor** offers information on the regulations concerning using employees in your home business and booklets such as "Employment Relationships Under the Fair Labor Standards Act." (202) 219-6666

10. **The Copyright Office,** Register of Copyrights
    Library of Congress
    Washington, D. C. 20559 (202) 479-0070
    The Copyright Office offers free publications on copyrights, trademarks, etc.

11. **Patent and Trademark Office**
    U.S. Department of Commerce
    Washington, DC 20231
    703) 557-INFO for information and publications on obtaining patents and trademarks for your product.

12. **State Department of Agriculture:** Under the U. S. Department of Agriculture, Agricultural Cooperative Services, Washington, DC 20250, your State Department of Agriculture is the place for information regarding food and cooking-related businesses. They provide information on labelling jars, Health Department requirements, and marketing products in each state. Often home-based business people avoid the agencies that can help them the most, like this one, that can be a great source for networking.

13. **State Health Department,** City and County Health Departments provide information on requirements to set up food-related businesses; lease out approved kitchen for producing your food product, etc.

14. **National Assocation for the Self-Employed**
    2121 Precinct Line Road
    Hurst, Texas 76054   (800) 232-NASE
    NASE offers group medical and dental insurance for home and small-business owners, a newsletter, *Self-Employed America,* business consulting, discounts on travel, prescriptions, office supplies, and other services and products.

15. American Home Sewing Association, Dept. SN
    1375 Broadway, 4th Floor
    New York, NY 10018

16. Hobby Industry Association of America
    319 E. 54th Street
    Elmwood, NJ 07407
    Offers a schedule of all craft and hobby trade shows
    nationwide, plus valuable information for those in the hobby
    and craft industry.

17. Greeting Card Association
    1350 New York Avenue, N.W.
    Suite 615
    Washington, DC 120005

18. National Association of Desktop Publishers
    462 Old Boston Road
    Topsfield, MA 01983

19. National Association for the Specialty Food Trade
    8 W. 40th Street
    New York, NY 10018-3902

20. Inventors Workshop International Education Foundation
    3201 Corte Malpase, Suite 304
    Camarillo, CA 93011

21. National Association of Women Business Owners
    1337 K Street NW
    Washington, DC 20005
    (301) 608-2590

Appendix B

State Home-Based Business Associations

The following states have state Home-Based Business Associations, with educational opportunities, publications, and resources. The State, District and Local meetings of Home-Based Business Associations are excellent sources of information on business management, but also provide networking opportunities:

Colorado

Aurora Small Business Development Center
9905 E. Colsax
Aurora, CO 80010
303-341-4849

Missouri

Community Development Specialist
Associated Electric Cooperative
Box 754
Springfield, MO 65801
314-634-2454

Nebraska

Nebraska Home-Based Business
P. O. Box 2136
Kearney, NE 68848
(308) 236-5454

California

Home Office and Business Opportunities
92 Corporate Ste. C-250
Irving, CA 92714
(714) 261-9474

Oklahoma

Central Office for Home-Based Entrepreneurship
HES 135, Oklahoma State University
Stillwater, OK 74078
(405) 744-5776

Pennsylvania

The Office Annex
Suite 720-Two Gateway Center
Pittsburg, PA 15222
(412) 355-0480

South Dakota

East River Electric Power Cooperative
P. O. Drawer E
Madison, SD 57042
(605) 256-4536

For states wanting to establish a home-based business association, a guide for states is available. Contact: Director, Central Office for Home-Based Entrepreneurship, HES 135, Oklahoma State University, Stillwater, OK 74078.

Appendix C

On-Line Service:
Forums, Research, Databases and
Marketing

- SBA Online is the electronic bulletin board of the Small Business Administration. Several SBA publications can be accessed via SBA Online. To connect with SBA Online for small or home business management support, call 1-900-463-4636.

- "Working From Home" Forum on *Compuserve,* featuring Paul and Sarah Edwards. Opportunities for networking on-line, gaining information, business advice, and ideas for service and product-based businesses.

- Free 10 hours online service available from these providers. Each online service has forums, databases, research and marketing resources for small and home-based businesses:

America OnLine 1-800-827-6364
Compuserve 1-800-848-8199
GEnie 1-800-638-9636
Prodigy 1-800-776-3449

Local and regional providers of online services:
check Yellow Pages

Appendix D

Directories

Directories are a good source of information on a variety of topics of interest to home-based businesses such as U.S. and world marketing data and statistics, trade shows worldwide, U.S. and European wholesalers, publishers, etc. Directories are expensive ($90 to $500). Reference sections of libraries contain directories, and much directory information can be accessed online in databases. The following is a sampling of the many directories available which are useful to home businesses:

- Gale Research Company, 835 Penobscot Bldg., 645 Griswold St., Detroit, MI 48226 (313) 961-2242 or (800) 877-4253:
- *Newsletters in Print,* 1994–1995 details more than 11,500 newsletters.
- *Encyclopedia of Associations*
- *Trade Shows Worldwide, 1995*
- *Trade Shows and Professional Exhibits Directory*
- *Ward's Business Directory*
- *Inventing and Patenting Sourcebook*
- *Business Plans Handbook*
- *American Wholesalers and Distributors Directory*
- *National Directory of Mailing Lists, 1995*
- Other useful directories include:
- *Standard Rate and Data Service, Inc.* 3002 Glenview Rd., Wilmette, IL 60091 (800 323-4588.
- *Editor and Publisher Market Guide,* a guide to U.S. and Canadian newspapers and newspaper groups. The Editor and Publisher Company, 11 W. 19th Street, NY, NY 10011.
- *Books in Print* (most libraries have in Reference Section)
- *Broadcasting Yearbook.* Reed Reference Publishing, (800) 521-8110.

Appendix E

Newsletters and Periodicals

Cheapskate Monthly, Mary Hunt, Editor.
P. O. Box 2135
Paramount, CA 90723-8135
310) 630-8845

Healthy Exchanges, Joanna Lund, Editor
P. O. Box 124
DeWitt, Iowa 52742-0124
319) 659-8234

GiftBasket News, Gift Basket Network Association
9655 Chimney Hill Lane,
Suite 1036
Dallas, Texas 75243(
214) 690-1917

National Home Business Report, Barbara Brabec, Editor
P. O. Box 2138
Naperville, IL 60566

Homeworking Mothers, Mothers' Home Business Network
P. O. Box 423
East Meadow, NY 11554
(516) 997-7394

Bits & Pieces (monthly newsletter containing common sense,
ideas, and practical advice on working with people)
Economics Press
12 Daniel Road
Fairfield, NJ 07004-9987
(800) 526-2554

The Entrepreneurial Spirit, Doug Kipp, Editor
#125, 339-10 Avenue, SE
Calgary, Alberta, Canada
T2G OW2
(403) 255-9387

Telecommuting Report
Electronic Services Unlimited
79 Fifth Avenue
New York, NY 10003

Craft Marketing News, The Front Room Publishers
P. O. Box 1541
Clifton, NJ 07015

Success: The Magazine for Today's Entrepreneurial Mind
P. O. Box 3036
Harlan, Iowa 51593-2097

Entrepreneur

P. O. Box 57050
Irvine, CA 92619

Craft Supply Magazine:
The Independent Journal for the Professional Crafter,
Tammy Keck, Editor
225 Gordons Corner Plaza
P. O. Box 420
Manolopan, NJ 07726

Threads Magazine
The Taunton Press, Inc.,
63 S. Main Street
P. O. Box 5506
Newtown, CT 06470-5506

Home Office Computing
730 Broadway
New York, NY 10003

Business Week
P. O. Box 506
Hightstown, NJ 08320

References

1 –p.11

Home Business Report newsletter, Easton, Pennsylvania

2 –p.41

Adapted from *Home-Based Business: Legal Consideration* published by Oklahoma Cooperative Extension Service, Oklahoma State Univerity, Stillwater, Oklahoma, p.5.

3 –p.45

Funk and Wagnall's New International Dictionary of the English Language, Newark, New Jersey, Publishers International Press, 1982, p.1330.

4 –p.45

Brabec, Barbara, *Homemade Money,* Whitehall, Virginia, Betterway Publications, Inc., 1989, p.126.

5 –p.65

Warren, Rick, *Fax of Life,* Mission Viejo, California, Self-published, April 21, 1995.

6 –p.77

Adapted from *Home-Based Business: Putting It All Together,* Cooperative Extension Service, Oklahoma State University, Stillwater, Oklahoma. Used by persmission.

7 –p.143

Edwards, Paul and Sarah, *Working From Home,* New York, G. P. Putman's Sons, 1994, p.518.

8 –p.173

Warren, Rick, March 17, 1995

9 –p.176

The Wall Street Journal, Vol. XCI #123, SW Edition, June 25, 1993, p.B1.

10 –p.184

O'Connor, Lindsey, *Working At Home,* Eugene, Oregon, Harvest House Publishers, 1990, p.156.

11 –p.187

O'Connor, Lindsey, p.166.

Index

Other Books by Starburst Publishers
(Partial listing—full list available on request)

Home Business Happiness   —Cheri Fuller

Subtitled: *Secrets On Keeping The Family Ship Afloat From Entrepreneurs Who Made It*. More than 26 million people in the U.S. work at home businesses. **Home Business Happiness** is your network for success! In a reader-friendly style. Author Cheri Fuller offers valuable advice from some of the most inventive and pioneering entrepeneurs in the country. Some of the topics included are: Starting a Home Business, Time Management, and Avoiding Potential Pitfalls.

(trade paper) ISBN 0914984705   **$12.95**

The Crystal Clear Guide to Sight
—Gayton & Ledford

Subtitled: *A Complete Manual of Eye Care for Those Over 40*. **The Crystal Clear Guide to Sight For Life** makes eye care easy-to-understand by giving clear knowledge of how the eye works with the most up-to-date information available from the experts. Contains more than 40 illustrations, a detailed index for cross-referencing, a concise glossary, and answers to often-asked questions. This book takes much of the guesswork out of eye problems, alleviates fear and apprehension often experienced by patients, when medical problem develops.

(trade paper) ISBN 0914984683   **$15.95**

God's Vitimin "C" for the Spirit
—Kathy Collard Miller & D. Larry Miller

Subtitled: *"Tug-at-the-Heart" Stories to Fortify and Enrich Your Life. Includes inspiring stories and anecdotes that emphasize Christian ideals and values by Barbara Johnson, Billy Graham, Nancy L. Dorner, Dave Dravecky,* Patsy Clairmont, Charles Swindoll, H. Norman Wright, Adell Harvey, Max Lucado, James Dobson, Jack Hayford and many other well-known Christian speakers and writers. Topics include: Love, Family Life, Faith and Trust, Prayer, Marriage, Relationships, Grief, Spiritual Life, Perseverance, Christian Living, and God's Guidance.

(trade paper) ISBN 091494837   **$12.95**

God's Chewable Vitamin "C" for the Spirit

Subtitled: *A Dose of God's Wisdom One Bite at a Time*. A collection of inspirational Quotes and Scriptures by many of your favorite Christian speakers and writers. It will motivate your life and inspire your spirit. You will *chew* on every *bite* of wisdom from *God's Chewable Vitamin "C" for the Spirit*.

(trade paper) ISBN 0914984845   **$6.95**

From Grandma With Love
—Ann Tuites

Subtitled: *Thoughts for Her Children Everywhere.* People are taught all kinds of things from preschool to graduate school, but they are expected to know instinctively how to get along with their families. Harmony within the home is especially difficult when an aging relative is involved. The author presents personal anecdotes to encourage caregivers and those in need of care. Practical, emotional and spiritual support is given so that all generations can learn to live together in harmony.

(hardcover) ISBN 0914984616 **$14.95**

Migraine—Winning the Fight of Your Life
—Charles Theisler

This book describes the hurt, loneliness and agony that migraine sufferers experience and the difficulty they must live with. It explains the different types of migraines and their symptoms, as well as the related health hazards. Gives 200 ways to help fight off migraines, and shows how to experience fewer headaches, reduce their duration, and decrease the agony and pain involved.

(trade paper) ISBN 0914984632 **$10.95**

Parenting With Respect and Peacefulness
—Louise A. Dietzel

Subtitled: *The Most Difficult Job in the World.* Parents who love and respect themselves parent with respect and peacefulness. Yet, parenting with respect is the most difficlult job in the world. This book informs parents that respect and peace communicate love—creating an atmosphere for children to maximize their development as they feel loved, valued, and safe. Parents can learn authority and control by commonsense, interpersonal, and practical approaches to day-to-day issues and situations in parenting.

(trade paper) ISBN 0914984667 **$10.95**

The World's Oldest Health Plan
—Kathleen O'Bannon Baldinger

Subtitled: *Health, Nutrition and Healing from the Bible.* Offers a complete health plan for body, mind and spirit, just as Jesus did. It includes programs for diet, exercise and mental health. Contains foods and recipes to lower cholesterol and blood pressure, improve the immune system and other bodily functions, reduce stress, reduce or cure constipation, eliminate insomnia, reduce forgetfulness, confusion and anger, increase circulation and thinking ability, eliminate "yeast" problems, improve digestion, and much more.

(trade paper-opens flat) ISBN 0914984578 **$14.95**

Books by Starburst Publishers—cont'd.

Dr. Kaplan's Lifestyle of the Fit & Famous   —Eric Scott Kaplan

Subtitled: *A Wellness Approach to "Thinning and Winning."* A comprehensive guide to the formulas and principles of: FAT LOSS, EXERCISE, VITAMINS, NATURAL HEALTH, SUCCESS and HAPPINESS. More than a health book—it is a lifestyle based on the empirical formulas of healthy living. Dr. Kaplan's food-combining principles take into account all the major food sources (fats, proteins, carbohydrates, sugars, etc.) that when combined within the proper formula (e.g. proteins cannot be mixed with refined carbohydrates) will increase metabolism and decrease the waistline. This allows you to eat the foods you want, feel great, and eliminate craving and binging.

(hard cover) ISBN 091498456X   **$21.95**

Allergy Cooking With Ease   —Nicolette M. Dumke

Subtitled: *The No Wheat, Milk, Eggs, Corn, Soy, Yeast, Sugar, Grain, and Gluten Cookbook.* A book designed to provide a wide variety of recipes to meet many different types of dietary and social needs and, whenever possible, save you time in food preparation. Includes: Recipes for those special foods that most food allergy patients think they will never eat again; Timesaving tricks; and Allergen Avoidance Index.

(trade paper-opens flat) ISBN 091498442X   **$12.95**

Purchasing Information:

Books are available from your favorite Bookstore, either from current stock or special order. To assist bookstore in locating your selection be sure to give title, author, and ISBN #. If unable to purchase from the bookstore you may order direct from STARBURST PUBLISHERS. When ordering enclose full payment plus $3.00 for shipping and handling ($4.00 if Canada or Overseas). Payment in US Funds only. Please allow two to three weeks minimum (longer overseas) for delivery. Make checks payable to and mail to STARBURST PUBLISHERS, P.O. Box 4123, LANCASTER, PA 17604. Credit card orders may also be placed by calling 1-800-441-1456 (credit card orders only), Mon-Fri, 8 AM–5 PM Eastern Time. **Prices and availability subject to change without notice.** 1-96